the lights
of *Mahonri*
MORIANCUMER

the lights
of *Mahonri*
MORIANCUMER

by PHYLLIS GUNDERSON

CFI

Springville, Utah

ISBN 13: 978-1-59955-019-0

Published by CFI, an imprint of Cedar Fort, Inc., 2373 W. 700 S., Springville, UT, 84663
Distributed by Cedar Fort, Inc. www.cedarfort.com

LIBRARY OF CONGRESS CATALOGING-IN-PUBLICATION DATA

    Gunderson, Phyllis.
     The lights of Mahonri Moriancumer / Phyllis Gunderson.
      p. cm.
     ISBN-13: 978-1-59955-019-0
     1. Women archaeologists--Fiction. 2. Older Mormons--Fiction. 3. Mormon
women--Fiction. [1. Book of Mormon--Fiction.] I. Title.
     PS3607.U5475L54 2007
     813'.6--dc22
                  2006100000

Cover design by Nicole Williams
Cover design © 2007 by Lyle Mortimer
Edited and typeset by Kammi Rencher

Printed in the United States of America

10 9 8 7 6 5 4 3 2 1

Printed on acid-free paper

CHAPTER I

We reached for the same book at the same time, high on a dusty shelf of a library in Bangkok. I almost grinned when he removed his hand before it could touch mine. I'd seen him search through books at the end of the aisle and recognized the orange robes and shaved head of a Buddhist Monk. If he touched me, a woman, he'd have to go through a purification ritual—maybe a walk on hot coals or have pins stuck under a few fingernails. I really didn't know. Someday I'd have to ask. I knew only that he wouldn't arm-wrestle me for the book and that it was now mine by default. I lowered it from the shelf and was rewarded with a shower of dust. Obviously, no one had been curious about this volume for at least a decade. Now suddenly there were two of us who had some purpose in its contents. If I were a decent sort of person I'd offer to give him the book, but . . . oh, well.

"I see we are to having the same interest," he said with a tiny bow of his bald head. He spoke with a crisp, proper British accent but the grammar was Asian. He was close to my age, perhaps in his sixties. With those oriental genes he could be a centenarian and still look younger than me. Even his hair would be black if it hadn't been shaved. Some things in this world aren't fair.

I joined him in the nod of heads and said, "You're looking for ancient Babylonian legends?"

"I am find *Epic of Gilgamesh*," he said. "I do not to know other of what you say."

"Yes. Well, actually, the Epic is found all over the Middle East, from ancient Sumer to Babylon to . . ." there wasn't a spark of recognition, and I wondered if he knew what he was looking for. "Why are you interested in Gilgamesh?"

"I am . . . was . . . being told of lights that do not die."

"Lights that don't die? In the Gilgamesh Epic?" I mentally reviewed what I remembered of the lengthy legend, a massive collection of mythological adventures involving two friends, Gilgamesh and Enkidu. When Enkidu dies, Gilgamesh is so grieved he refuses to allow burial of his friend until a worm crawls out the nose. Then Gilgamesh goes on a quest for eternal life and is guided to the home of the gods where he interviews a guy named Utnapishtim, the Babylonian version of Noah. The whole flood story shows up, including a few details of the ark.

"Ahhhh," I said, "the ark of Noah. Maybe the Epic mentions lights on Noah's ark, but I don't remember it."

"You are also interesting in lights?"

"Not really. I want to review the Epic for a class I teach." *Okay*, I thought, *this old guy is making small talk with a woman. He doesn't intend to go away without the book, the only English copy in multiple libraries. If I study it here, he'll retreat to another table and watch until I've finished.* There was an almost desperate hunger in his eyes and I knew, even though I regretted it already, I'd end up giving Gilgamesh to the monk—but not until I found out what was behind his need to know. How many Buddhist monks make Babylonian legends part of their leisure reading? There was a plot unfolding here. I like plots. And I like mysteries. And even though I don't like people very much, I put up with them because you can't have plots and mysteries without them. This old monk was engaging, and his English was good enough to be understood.

"I want to read this book," I said, "but I'm more interested in why you want to read it. Would you consider a trade? This book for your story?"

The man leaned his head toward his draped shoulder and looked as if he were listening to a voice inside himself, giving permission to speak. "I will tell at you," he decided. We moved to a long, empty table in a corner of the room. I sat opposite him with the table between us, careful not to touch his robes with my knees. He had gathered the fabric around him as a precaution, but I was extra thoughtful in the seating arrangement so he'd be at ease.

"Let's start at the very beginning," I said.

"A very good place to start," he grinned. "I learn 'Doe, a Deer' song when I study English at monastery."

I laughed aloud, right there in the dusty Bangkok library.

"My name was Mahi . . ." he began.

CHAPTER 2

"M y name was Mahi. Tibet was my country before
all become lost. At age twelve year, I am living
at monastery to be study as novice monk. I and my
friend . . ."

The story was like the unfolding of a long piece of
cloth, a pattern woven with gentle words in the wrong
place, but comprehensible with each unfolding. They were
like two little boys anywhere in the world, except they
were wrapped in long, saffron-colored robes that kept
tripping them. Scrambling across the rocks behind the
monastery, they headed toward an outcropping at the top
of the mountain, outlined by a diffuse sun rising above
the crest. As shadows met light, a crevice resembled an
open door. Intrigued, the young novice monks climbed to
investigate, their faded orange habits tucked between their
legs and held with one hand as the other hand searched
for holds in the rock.

"The end is farther than it first looked."

"But we will continue and reach the goal."

A day off from the demands of the Lamasery was rare.
They were grateful to the Masters for protection, religious
instruction, and practical education, but oh, how delicious

to feel the cool breeze kiss their ears and the mist dampen their shaved heads.

"Mahi, I've lost sight of the door."

"You looked down at your hands?"

Sherup smiled. "True. I forgot the teaching and used my eyes to find holds in the rocks."

"Eyes always on the goal," Mahi quoted. "Leave your body to feel its way."

Sherup searched the edge of light and dark to rediscover the door, but it was gone. He knew it would not appear to his vision again. Mahi was their hope. The slope gently leveled and they walked easily for a time.

"Mahi, have you left your body yet?" It was a question Sherup would never ask during chores at the monastery. But here, as they concentrated on a common goal, it seemed any subject could be discussed without concern. "I mean, I know it is not allowed until we are older, but haven't you tried?"

"I have thought of it," Mahi returned. "The danger of doing such a thing without a Master is foolish. I hear an apprentice made the attempt once. His body still waits in a locked room while his spirit wanders the nether world without a guide. It took place before we came."

"I would like to see such a body," Sherup replied with contempt. "It is a story to frighten boys."

A steep incline kept the young monks breathing too hard for idle conversation. Sherup's eleven-year-old legs scrambled to stay on top of the small avalanche of rocks dislodged by Mahi, who was several feet above. Mahi held his gaze through the changing lights of sun and shade, feeling his way over boulders, until he finally balanced on top of an outcropping.

"This is it," he called to his friend, still laboring below.

"I see no door," Sherup said with disappointment. "It was only the *maya* of this world, an illusion."

"No," Mahi answered with a grin. "The illusion is that no door exists."

As Sherup watched, Mahi melted into the cliff and disappeared. Seen from the front, the cliff wall looked flat and solid. But as Sherup struggled the last few yards he saw the gap Mahi had slipped through. The width could accommodate a grown man, as long as he was only five feet tall and slender. The two boys, aged eleven and twelve, novice monks who didn't eat much, easily entered the narrow passage which immediately made a sharp turn, then another, and another. They groped in darkness until they noticed a kind of twilight, making it possible to see. The ceiling widened to join the mountain wall as the boys crept around the rock corner of the short labyrinth.

They had entered a wide chamber with a floor-to-ceiling door at the end made of two smooth metal panels. Sherup joined Mahi at the door, which was so large that three men could stand on each other's shoulders and walk through. It was wide enough for five yaks to enter side by side. But the sight that held the boys mesmerized was a stream of light escaping through a two-inch slit in the center of the door, splashing across the dirt at their feet and running up the rock wall behind them. The luminous silver light came from inside the mountain.

"Why would a mountain have light?" Mahi whispered. "There cannot be such a thing. Even at the monastery, butter lamps do not burn so bright. This could not be done with a hundred butter lamps."

Sherup didn't bother to analyze the situation and pushed ahead, peeking through the slightly open door as Mahi gasped.

"You'll be blinded."

"No. The light doesn't hurt my eyes. Oh, Mahi! Such things of wonder."

"What do you see?"

"Great pieces of . . . I don't know. Things made by hands, but surely not those of our Masters. Come and see. The light is gentle."

They gingerly squeezed around the door into an immense cavern, larger than the entire dining area of the monastery. Higher than the tower at the Potala. Bigger than the audience room and assembly hall combined. Twice bigger than the great Cathedral of Lhasa. The cave was full of mechanical monsters fashioned from a dark silver metal, so smooth it seemed to shine. The ancient machinery reflected light high above them. With heads bent back, the boys studied several smooth globes hanging from the domed ceiling. They could gaze directly as if at moonlight, yet the brightness illuminated details of the room without the flickering shadows of fire.

Cave exploration was done carefully at first, in respectful awe of the massive metal objects filling the room. But, true to their ages, the youths soon ran from one device to another, calling greetings and counting how long it took the echo to return.

Against a far wall was a great statue, the body of a cat with a woman's face and shoulders. Skillfully crafted eyes seemed to watch the boys as they explored, and, uncomfortably aware of the stone woman's stare, they moved to the opposite side of the cavern. Display cases held miniature models of cities, pyramids, more cats with human heads, and curious items small enough to fit in a hand. A metal box with spectacles attached intrigued Mahi and he placed his face against it. The glasses, spaced too far for his small face, required him to squint one eye and place the other against an eyepiece, his hands resting on something similar to bicycle handles. Inside, the box came alive with moving pictures of men inhabiting a very different world from the one familiar to the boys. The scenes were three dimensional and so green that they bordered on blue, inhabited by unknown animals and marvels of scientific progress. Vehicles glided inches from the surface or miles above it. Temple pinnacles pushed into the clouds. Giant pyramids dotted the landscape, with people leaving and entering as if the pyramids were apartment buildings. Cities floated on seas. Aircraft hovered in one place and then flashed to another with amazing speed.

Mahi jerked his head back. Motion pictures had been developed at the turn of the century, but even in the early 1950s Mahi had not yet seen such things for himself. He wondered if there were tiny people living in the box and checked behind the rectangular enclosure, soon realizing the extensive world he saw couldn't fit inside. Again he adjusted his eye to the eyepiece, and the scenes started over. Soon the picture changed to conflict, warfare, a vivid flash in the sky, then another, and a city vanished into gas. Above the ruins rose a red cloud, the shape of a mushroom. Green forests turned from trees to ash in an eye-blink.

The picture faded, replaced by a group of people excavating the cavern the boys were now exploring, using immense machines to cut the rock, filling the space with records and artifacts of their civilization. Mahi saw the crystal globes being lifted into place by a man standing on a platform that moved rapidly up, down, and sideways. A change in the picture showed white vapor streaking across blue skies, then the heavens turned red. The world trembled and shook; cities burst into flame and were gone. Great chasms opened in the earth, belching floods that covered mountains. A wave higher than the tallest buildings swept across the land.

Suddenly, a scream. Mahi first thought the sound came from the scenes he was watching but soon realized the calls for help came from outside the box. He pulled his head away and looked around the cavern. Sherup had stepped on a platform, three feet square with guardrails, attached to yet another machine by a long, folded metal tube. The platform shuddered with life to take a shocked and frightened Sherup thirty feet into the air. By the time Mahi reached the spot the metal tube had completely unfolded and swung toward a sphere of light. Sherup looked ashen, desperately clinging to the railings.

"Sherup!" Mahi yelled, "drop to the floor so you won't be burned by the lamp."

Sherup flattened himself to the flooring and covered his head with his arms as the platform halted beneath the globe. A short silence later, he lifted his head and looked at the light, then stood and reached out to it.

"What are you doing!" cried Mahi.

Sherup touched the round light source. "There's no heat," he said. "In fact, it's cold like the mountain streams of thawing."

"Look for a button or lever to use. Maybe that will bring you down." Mahi analyzed the situation. The metal tube was too far away for Sherup to safely slide down. Falling from that height would kill him. Mahi tried to stay calm and wait for the solution to present itself, as the Masters had taught. The waiting was short. Another tremor animated the platform as it moved to its original position and descended. Sherup jumped from the metal monster before it touched the ground, fearing the evil thing would change its mechanical mind and fly upwards again. The boys stared at each other.

"We must report this to a Master." Mahi, older by a year, felt the responsibility of his station and was concerned about the close call they had experienced. But Sherup lovingly touched one of the metal behemoths, leaned his weight against it and explored the smooth surface with his palm before he spoke.

"There is no hurry," he said. "We could keep this our secret for awhile. We could come here during our times of solitude and discover answers to this mystery." He faced Mahi. "The sun itself showed us the way. True, you kept your eyes on the goal while I looked aside, but I followed you. This place belongs to us."

Mahi stood resolute.

"Please, Mahi. Let us have this for a small time."

Mahi shook his head. "We must report this to a Master."

It took two days before any of the Masters could hold audience. The boys made the request the same day they slid down the mountain, but no one took seriously two novice trainees with something of "great importance" to tell. It was the venerable Lama Rampa who finally sat before them, hands folded, his bald head sitting tall on a straight back, the skin between his clavicle and shoulder sunk deep enough to hold a small lemon. The boys bowed their heads to the floor, bottoms high in the air. When they rose to a kneeling position, Rampa fought to control the smile that formed.

"You have requested audience for a purpose of great importance," he said. "It is an honor to hear your petition."

"Master," Mahi began, "We have discovered a mystery in the mountain behind the Lamasery."

"The mysteries of existence are found everywhere," Lama Rampa encouraged. "Could you identify such a thing?" The old monk expected the boys had found an animal, dead or alive, that had not been encountered before.

"No sir, we cannot explain what we have found. We have never seen such objects created by the hand of man and could not identify a purpose, but there was light where there should be no light. A light that continued without failing. That, too, we have not seen before."

The old Lama's eyes narrowed. "Perhaps you should tell me the exact spot where you beheld these forbidden mysteries."

Forbidden. It was an inauspicious word that spoke many meanings. The little monks described their climb to the door-shaped shadow, the cleverly concealed shaft leading to a large metal door without handles, a light radiating from the slightly open entrance. Rampa studied each child as the story unfolded.

"And you say the cavern was lit by light softer than the sun, its source several globes hanging from the ceiling." It was not a question.

"Yes, Master," Sherup said. "It is a cavern of great wonders. We believe the Masters will know the answer."

Rampa was quiet. The boys had learned not to fidget during the silence of the monks. They remained in upright kneeling position, heads bent, hands in prayer position under their chins, waiting for the master to speak.

"You have seen what you should not, and which few have looked upon. The open door will be discussed with the Gomchens and will not happen again."

So Gomchens, hermits living in the mountains, knew about the cave and were somehow responsible for the door. Sherup timidly asked the question most important to him.

"Will we be allowed to see the cave once more?"

"You will not." Sherup's small body sunk as the old monk continued. "The contents of the cave are not your calling. If you speak of your discovery to anyone, your training here will be terminated. You will be returned to your village and the poverty of your parents."

The boys knew such an event would bring shattering disgrace. When they'd been chosen to serve at the monastery, it had been a time of celebration and thanksgiving. If they were sent home, they would be the shame of their families and would spend the rest of their lives plowing fields. They could not jeopardize this opportunity, but their disappointment was keen.

It was Mahi who made the request. "Might we know the mystery? Would you give us knowledge?"

"I think you will search forever, but you will never find answers unless I tell you." The old man bowed his head as if praying. Mahi and Sherup remained patient as their training had taught them, and when the monk raised his eyes again, he said solemnly, "I will tell you." In a tumble of thank-yous and other words of gratitude, the novices bowed repeatedly until the Master halted the display.

"You will ask no questions for I will give no answers beyond what you receive today." The youths were silent as the venerable Rampa began.

"The Cave of the Ancients is the reason our monastery was built on this site. We guard the secret until the time comes to reveal it. Only the rishis and monks of this monastery are aware of it, but of course you have now seen. I myself was taken to see it when but a boy, like you, because my work in the world made it fitting I should know of the cave. Did you find the room of darkness, where images form on the walls?"

"Sir," said Mahi, "I saw moving pictures in a box, but not a room."

"The story is told clearly from the room," the monk nodded his head and closed his eyes as if seeing the vision even now.

"The Ancients were a race of great accomplishment, but they relied on the work of their own hands rather than God. Eventually, they worshiped only their science and hate was spawned; wars were fought with machines of destruction; the skies rained death and weakened nature itself. Eventually, the earth took its revenge with great shakings and thunder; chasms unleashed floods, drowning the great race, burying their knowledge under mud created by forces of water both above and below. Caverns, such as the one you found, were designed by those who foresaw the end of their world. The repositories were meant for people of the future, if there were any survivors."

Mahi and Sherup hardly breathed for fear a noise or movement might end the story, but questions formed in their minds. How many caves were there? Why was this knowledge held secret? How often did the monks check the cave? Why was the door left open? Who decides when the world is ready for the technology contained in the cave?

Master Rampa continued. "The face of the earth changed, weather patterns altered, living plants and animals mutated, the years of men were shortened. Survivors began a primitive existence, forgetting the machines in the cavern. Our ancestors learned to live with the earth in its new condition, but memories of the flood remained, along with legends of a man who saved animals in a very large ship. Jews have a book that speaks of Noah. Babylon kept the same legend telling of Utnapishtim. Sumerians wrote of Zisudra, and in Central America he is Tezpi. Greeks call their flood hero Deucalion . . ." Rampa took a deep breath, as if wondering how much information could be shared. Then he continued.

"There are four known time capsules: one buried in the sands of Egypt, another beneath a pyramid in South America, a third in Siberia, and our own Cave of the Ancients in Tibet."

The boys sat silent.

When Rampa spoke again it was more to himself than to his small audience.

"The lights in the cave above this monastery have been shining for many thousands of years. It is a marvel of ancient attainment, radiance from a crystal rock to produce cold light. The process, according to legend, used an inert radioactive substance and required nine years of intense heat."

Mahi stared in awe at the old man, who had lived in the western world and knew much. But Mahi didn't think such lights could be made even in the West. He gathered courage to speak. "You said there would be a time when . . ."

"There will be no questions," the old monk interrupted. "And no more answers. You are excused."

CHAPTER 3

I looked at Mahi the monk, wondering what parts of his story I could believe and how much he'd invented so he could get the Epic of Gilgamesh. I was hardly an expert about people and their motivations, but this monk 'felt' honest to me, and his eyes held steady.

"Did you and Sherup return to the cave?"

"Lama Rampa give at us many works to keep us away to the cave." I loved the way he fractured English. It was a joy to listen to him. The old man who was once a young Mahi continued.

"After days of thirty, maybe more, we climbing to cave for one seeing. We are saying, each to each, 'The promise was never to speak of cave, but it is no breaking to look again.' We must to search a long time for the door. When we find, it is closed and center have the cement."

"The door was sealed," I repeated. "I guess the monks decided the world wasn't ready for a prehistoric technological civilization. And you've been looking for more information about the lights ever since?"

"No, no," he smiled. "I am never to talking again of Cave of Ancients. I desire to finish the training, I am being a monk, leave Tibet before soldiers kill. I am . . . was . . .

following Dalai Lama to India, then come to Thailand. Now I teach tourist at Wat Mahathat. I am to give meditation teaching for tourist because I speak the English."

"It is a job good for you," I said, finding myself using his speech pattern, as if he weren't capable of understanding anything else. Here I am, an old lady, and I still talk before I think.

"Your English is easy to understand," I finished. Then, curious, I asked, "What happened to your friend, Sherup?"

"He is being dead," Mahi answered. "He was at monastery when soldiers come."

I hated that part of recent history when Communist China took Tibet in the 1950s. The event happened in my lifetime while I bought strawberry milkshakes at "Big D" and listened to rock and roll, totally unaware because the doors of China were locked. Then, in the 1970s, President Nixon arranged a cultural exchange of ping-pong teams. The Chinese easily beat the Americans, a fortunate event which may have helped open Communist China to further contact with the West.

I heard the Chinese side of the Tibetan story while working with a western crew at a site south of Xiamen. Our interpreter explained that the war with Tibet was exactly like the American Civil War. One side tried to leave the union and the other side stopped them. It was a clever argument and there wasn't much to say after that, so we didn't. The escape of the Dalai Lama provides one of the great adventure stories of the century. Too bad Sherup had not been so fortunate.

"I'm sorry to hear about Sherup," I said.

"Do not mourn," my monk said kindly. "I believe he is learn to keep eye on goal and let body be alone. If he did not to reach Nirvana yet, he is born monk again. All is well."

Mahi the Monk folded his hands on his robe beneath the table and waited. I picked up the hint.

"Well," I said, "it was a good trade. You get the book first." I pushed the Epic to the center of the table and removed my hand so my monk could touch the book without defilement.

"I will be to thank you," he said as he stood.

"Why did you want an English version of Gilgamesh?" I asked.

"I am taught to reading Tibetan and Sanskrit and English," he said. "But cannot to read Thai."

It would, of course, be easier to find an English translation than Sanskrit. For some reason I hated to see him go; there was more to say, more to learn, so I formed more questions.

"Where did you hear about the Epic of Gilgamesh?"

"Tourist at Wat. He is try to make of me a Christian. We talk of Jew Bible, he tell of Noah and flood. I tell of flood in Tibet, but not of cave. He tell of Gilgamesh and flood, and say lights in ark of Noah are in story. Then I am wanting to read."

He smiled and nodded. I smiled and nodded. It was over.

After he left, I followed him at a distance, thinking when he was finished I could pick up the book and do my research. At the main desk he stopped and produced a library card. He wasn't going to read the book at a table; he was taking it with him! Since I didn't own a card myself, it didn't occur to me that the book would be physically taken from the building. It could be weeks before I saw that book again, and I needed it now. I leaned in exasperation against a shelf, felt it shift, and stood straight before the whole load of books fell backwards. That's the last time I'll be Ms. Nice Guy. So much for gracious action, monk or no monk. Now what?

Okay, I'd start over, get an interpreter, use another Babylonian legend. But finding Gilgamesh in English had been difficult. What were the chances that more stories were here? I felt like swearing, but I maintain that people who swear are simply uneducated and don't know the right words to express frustration.

After two more hours in that dusty library, I ran out of proper words and swore.

The class turned out fine without Gilgamesh. I gave the lecture on young Champollion and how he deciphered the Rosetta Stone, a three-foot-nine-inch boulder discovered in Egypt in 1799. While other boys played ball in Paris streets, Champollion studied Greek and Egyptian Demotic, two of the three languages represented on the stone. At the age of nineteen he was head professor of languages at Grenoble, and at twenty-six became director of Egyptology at the Louvre. He died not long after he cracked the hieroglyphics and never learned what his mysterious Egyptians had to say. It's a tragic story. They loved it.

Students have to pass advanced English tests to sign up for my class, which is a combination of anthropology, archaeology, and practical English. My status as a visiting American professor does not require me to be good-looking, but when I walk into a class and introduce myself as Dr. Howard, there's initial surprise, if not disappointment. There I stand, a plump older woman, when they expected a handsome young man. To make atonement, I do what I can to be fascinating.

My name is Matt Howard.

Okay, it's Mathilda Howard, and I deeply resent my parents, wonderful though they were, for saddling me with a name like Mathilda. What were they thinking? I changed the name legally as soon as it could be done, about age eighteen as I remember. The deed was easy. As long as you make money, pay taxes, and hand over the fee, you can choose to call yourself Mickey Mouse. Matt Howard suits me.

I had a great childhood, a miserable youth, a pleasant prime, and now I'm in a terrific old age. Three out of four ain't bad. The miserable youth was because I was plain, overweight, and unacceptable. Good grades didn't help. The standard cruelty of peers pushed me into self-hatred. Not even the pimply, short, sharp-nosed boys asked me to dance.

I dissolved into ashes at high school but rose again after college. Not like the Phoenix bird with new life and bright plumage, but as myself, newly fascinated by the world and thrilled with discoveries of the ancient past. I jumped through the requisite hoops of ethnoarchaeology, a combination of anthropology and archaeology, spent nineteen years doing field work in unlikely places, and picked up a specialty in pottery dating. My rank was elevated, my tent private, and I became useful clear up to age forty. Then maternal urges took me to a Chinese orphanage where I found my daughter, Marisa, and brought her home. She was two years old.

Fieldwork wasn't practical for a single mother, so I switched to teaching and, eighteen years later, Marisa got married. Mo, her husband, gave me a hug on their wedding day.

"Thank you for bringing her across the world to me."

"Well, I didn't exactly have you in mind when I did it," I replied. "I think of you as a cat burglar who has stolen my prized possession."

He laughed, knowing my acidic humor wasn't meant to burn.

"Tell you what," he offered. "When you really need her back, I'll share. But only for a little while at a time."

"Mark," I said, because only Marisa called him Mo, "there may come a time you'll regret that offer because I'm not forgetting it."

With Marisa gone, teaching at foreign universities provided new experiences. India was my first assignment, Thailand my second. The demand was greater than I had time for. It's nice to be a scientist. We have authority, credibility, and power that extends to things we don't know anything about. People listen because we stand on the solid ground of evidence, not myth and legend. That's why the story of Mahi the monk preyed at the edges of my mind, pricked the boundaries, shadowed my surety. A civilization that preceded a mythical worldwide flood and produced eternal lights . . . it didn't fit any paradigm grid I knew.

The class at Chulalongkorn University came to a close and I prepared for the return home to Arizona. But I couldn't shake the monk's tale and needed to talk to Mahi again before leaving Thailand. What was the name of that temple where tourists were taught? Yes, downtown Bangkok, Wat Mahathat.

A tuk-tuk driver knew the place and left me in the street facing a long, narrow lane that connected with the next street a block away. I walked slowly past closed doors on both sides, assuming they hid empty cubicles, monk dormitories. The dirt lane and unpainted wood buildings were accented by brilliant bougainvilleas. The country was overgrown with wild reds and magentas in flowers that grew without tending. An open door on my right beckoned with English words, "Section Five. Meditation Training. Tourists Welcome." This was it.

Three stairs opened into a shabby room of rough plank floors and a multitude of posts holding the ceiling, bereft of décor. This was a no-nonsense establishment. A paunchy, middle-aged monk sat at a desk. I wondered how he could maintain his fat stores when he was only allowed to eat what he could beg during the morning. He welcomed me in English, the world's language.

"May I hell you?" he asked.

Thai people drop endings of words in their own language without a change in meaning. They can't be persuaded that English endings are important. I smiled in memory of the many times I'd been "helled" instead of helped.

"You have a monk here whose name was once Mahi. I don't know his monk name. He teaches meditation to tourists."

"You may go for finding," he invited.

Following the wave of his hand I entered a fire hazard of decrepit wooden chairs and tables leaning against walls. The smell of curry wafted through the air, accompanied by the clatter of dishes behind a door. It looked like this was once a dining room converted to a tourist trap that provided income for the monastery. Tourist contributions must have been worth the dislocation. On my right a young girl sporting a blond ponytail was dressed in the white robes of a female monk. She led a group of tourists, eyes closed, in walking meditation on a small, rickety stage. The setup was guaranteed to hurt somebody. I hoped the monastery had insurance for tourists who fell off the platform. The girl's instructions were spoken in American English and I yearned for her story, but the edge of my sight caught Mahi coming from the kitchen. With regret, I had to let the blonde girl fade away.

"Mahi?" I said. "I'd like to talk with you for just a minute."

"Ahhh, you are . . . person with Gilgamesh book?"

"Yes. Did you find what you were looking for in the *Epic of Gilgamesh*?"

"It is . . . was . . . book very big. I like many much. But no light of ark."

"There are a lot of old legends about the ark of Noah," I explained. "Maybe the Syrian version will help you. Even better, I remember Genesis in the Jewish Targum has God telling Noah to go to Pishon and get a precious stone to put in the ark for light." I warmed to the subject and got obnoxious. "The Hebrew word *tsohar* is sometimes translated as 'window,' but it also means 'a light-giving stone.' Rabbinic literature has a few things about the lights of the ark. There are a lot of sources for you to try." I stopped for air.

"It matters not," he bowed his head slightly. "In future day ancient writing will to give us all truth."

"The truth is what I'm here for," I replied. "I must know: Is your experience in the Cave of Ancients true? Did you see evidence of an advanced civilization we know nothing about? Was there really an eternal light?"

Mahi seemed surprised at the request and I felt embarrassed to doubt his integrity, but I pressed on.

"I *must* know," I said. My monk considered the question longer than was necessary. A simple yes or no would have sufficed. I was distinctly uncomfortable as he looked squarely into my eyes.

"All is true," he said.

I was on course toward drastic change.

CHAPTER 4

att, it's been too long since your fieldwork days."
John's voice sounded distant on the phone, as if I were
still in Bangkok instead of Arizona. He was emotionally
distant as well.

"I know, John, I know. But I've kept up with it,
teaching current techniques in class."

"I hate to put it this way, but . . . how old are you
now?"

I felt a bristling along my spine. John wasn't a spring
rooster himself. He'd once requested my presence at a dig
in Iraq where I'd identified a bulla used in an 8,000-year-
old counting system. The thing looked like a round clump
of clay and everybody had missed it, even John. I hadn't
been discreet about the clay ball's identity, and he'd never
quite forgiven me. Now, I changed the tone of my voice
to sound good-natured, which I could do because it was a
phone conversation. If John could have seen my face, he'd
have hid trembling in the bathroom.

"Does it matter how old I am?" I countered. "I can
stand upright and breathe in and out. My brain cell loss is
probably only a million a day. I still recognize a clay ball
from a bulla." Maybe I'd pushed that one too far.

"How old, Matt."

"Sixty, John. Still thirteen years younger than Gene Savoy, who putters through Peruvian jungles discovering Hebrew scripts and lost cities."

"But he's been consistent; he didn't take off and teach for, what, twenty years or so? You know the saying; you quoted it all the time. 'Those who can, do. Those who can't, . . .'"

"Teach," I finished for him. I was condemned by my own words. "Look, there has to be something coming up that needs a warm body. I want to get my hands dirty, feel the excitement of a find again. Don't write me off. Consider it."

"Right, Matt."

The return home to Arizona had been bittersweet. My little house in Scottsdale was lovely, purchased by my parents before the area became exclusive. It featured desert landscaping which didn't take much work or water, an interior design of mementos from a world of wonders, and pictures to remind me that life moves faster than opportunities. That was the bitter part. Parents, grandparents, and a daughter were all gone in one way or another. Marisa's wedding portraits hung on the wall.

There was a small jerk at my heart, and I turned away from her laughing eyes, determined to start moving in a different direction. The foreign professor stuff could be done in the future, but I really was getting old and there wasn't much time left for fieldwork. I drove to the university to check graduate bulletin boards for signs of action. Among all the worthless, time-wasting, insipid opportunities posted there, one caught my eye: a dig in its final stages on the east coast of China. They needed a group to finish the contract before the site opened for tourists, which proved that Communist China was learning how to use capitalism.

I called the phone number on top of the notice and introduced myself, my background, interests, and qualifications. The secretary on the phone rustled papers.

"We have a pottery specialist," she monotoned, "and don't need an ethnoarchaeologist."

"Well," I queried, "what do you still need?"

"Actually, we're looking for an interpreter who speaks Mandarin. The Chinese government won't be supplying one since the project is considered all but finished." The woman was getting gabby now. "It was started by our American team, but the Chinese need us to complete the contract so they can put together their tourist agenda with a Chinese team."

I tried to be sociable.

"It doesn't sound like the site could draw the same amount of tourists as the Terra Cotta Soldiers."

"This dig is prehistoric, two thousand years older than the soldier site in Xian. They hope to cash in on that. So, what we need is an interpreter."

"My daughter and I work as a team," I lied. "She's of Chinese descent and speaks fluent Mandarin."

A small pause at the other end.

"I'll connect you with Dr. Bausch, the project director."

I waited.

I waited some more.

"Dr. Howard," said the male voice, "in view of your experience we have room for you and your daughter."

There followed time schedules, fee schedules, questions and answers, but never interest in my age. Score one. When we hung up, a panic rose from my midsection. Marisa had indeed studied Mandarin. But fluent? Available? Willing? I was in trouble. I made the call to Chicago where she and Mark lived. Mark answered.

"Hey, Mark. It's your mother-in-law with news."

"Hey, Mom. I hope the news is good because my thesis is getting worse every day and I'm a grouch."

"Well, you could say, then, that it might be good news for both of us. Remember when you promised to share Marisa when I needed her?"

"When did I ever make a promise like that?"

"Mark! On your wedding day."

"C'mon. Everybody makes wild promises on their wedding day. Decent people forget about it."

"I'm not 'decent people,' and I'm collecting on this one. I'm taking Marisa out of your life for a few months while you finish your thesis." The last part was an afterthought, a little something to sweeten the deal.

Silence.

"I'll get Marisa."

I mentally rehashed all the convincing arguments. Enough time elapsed that I figured they were discussing it, and when Marisa finally answered, my rehearsed rebuttal came in hasty form.

"Come with me to China . . ."

"When . . .?"

" . . . It's a chance to use your Mandarin. All expenses paid with a little left over, and your resumé will be greatly enhanced. Play it right and it's worth university credit. You're on summer break now, we'll be together on an adventure, and Mark will finish his thesis without distraction, which is mainly you. Have I forgotten anything?"

"When do we leave?"

Bless her heart, my daughter is wonderful. Mark isn't bad, either. Our papers, shots, and passports were current because of my foreign travel and Marisa's honeymoon. We met the team at Dr. Bausch's university for a week of project training and were on the plane for Beijing.

For Marisa's twelfth birthday I had taken her to China so she could connect with her heritage. She saw the orphanage where I'd found her and whisked her away. We took a boat up the man-made Grand Canal, a thousand miles of hand-dug waterway still used for transport to Beijing. When we saw the Forbidden City, the sheer size left us stunned. We imagined its streets lined with ten thousand people living their royal lives in the walled complex. An old woman made her way carefully down the marble stairs, her feet too small to carry her safely, the result of fashionable foot binding as a child. Her wrinkled face was electric with wonder that she could breach those walls without a death penalty.

We saw notices tacked on walls prohibiting spitting on sidewalks, then watched an old man empty one nostril full of green goo in the middle of the road. Technically, it wasn't spitting. We raced each other across the Great Wall, stopping at the fortifications for breath. Now, nine years later, we found ourselves at an archaeology site three hundred miles south of Beijing.

The country was covered in fields of gold flowers, like a blanket on the world, its seeds destined to become bright yellow oil. When we arrived at the dig, the gold blanket was shredded. Dirt gouged from mother earth had been formed into small mounds, like chicken pox on her face.

Marisa and I helped raise tents, construct a Quonset hut kitchen to protect food stores, and set up tin-walled latrines over holes in the ground. She was beautiful, with shiny black hair so thick it stayed in place when she knotted it on top of her head. Her long legs lifted her to a five foot seven inch height and I suspected her natural father was probably Caucasian. Her dark almond eyes flashed when she was happy, angry, or frightened. I loved introducing her as my daughter, I could almost hear their thoughts: *How can she be your daughter when you're a short, squat little woman with inadequate mouse-gray hair, and she's tall, gorgeous, and Asian?* I figure it's blind luck.

The crew was less than standard size, and everyone did triple duty. Dr. Bausch was field director, administrative technician, and site supervisor. I became cataloguer, conservator, and assistant to the artifact analyst, a girl of about twenty-five. She knew she wouldn't be seeing much pottery on this trip. Marisa was considered a junior staff member, expected to communicate with the three-man crew of Chinese laborers we'd hired. Her first conversation with them sent her into peals of laughter. She explained her reaction later in our tent.

"What did they say that was so funny?" I asked.

"They wondered what a nice Chinese girl like me was doing with a bunch of 'big noses.'" She replied.

"Big noses!" I was offended that the work crew wasn't awed at our presence. "So that's what they call us behind our backs."

"They could insult you to your faces and, since none of you know Mandarin, it wouldn't matter," Marisa countered.

"They used the 'big nose' term because they thought you were one of them," I said.

"Well," she answered, raising her hands to the air, "they call 'em like they see 'em."

Then things got dry, dirty, slow, and boring, exactly

the way ninety-nine percent of all digs operate. It was beautiful.

Three weeks into the project the Chinese crew asked permission to visit a sacred mountain in the area and invited Marisa to go along, presumably because she was Chinese. I worried about her safety but didn't dare try 'mother-may-I' with a grown woman. That night Marisa was animated with excitement, waving her arms to express what she'd seen, moving, sitting, standing, moving again.

"Mom, you would not believe this mountain!"

I sat on a cot with chin in hands to prove she had my full attention.

"There's an ancient stairway carved right into it," she sat, knees crossed, leg wiggling. "It was amazing to see what primitive people could accomplish."

Yeah, yeah, yeah, I'd seen a thousand ancient stairs all over the world and stopped climbing them years ago. But the enthusiasm of youth is lovely so I asked questions.

"Did you get to the top?"

She stood. "Of course. Since I'm Chinese, the crew insisted I see the place, as if it should be part of my soul and I'd feel it if I got close enough. I think if I'd stopped climbing they would have carried me."

"*Did* you feel anything?"

Marisa laughed and crumpled to the floor. "I climbed six thousand steps to stand in an ancient temple with animal droppings on the floor. What I felt was exhausted, but it was impressive, and the Chinese chattered non-stop to explain it." She stood again and paced. "I think I nodded in the right places, but some of what they said didn't make sense. It was probably idiomatic vocabulary indigenous to the area." I loved it when she talked that way. Chip off the old block.

"Did they actually remember any history?" The Communists had destroyed just about every religious edifice during the 1960s Cultural Revolution, and I was amazed the stairs on a sacred mountain hadn't been hacked to pieces. Maybe destroying stairs wasn't a priority. They preferred shooting teachers.

"If I caught the story right," Marisa said, "they believed that before China became a great nation, when the land was empty, a large group of travelers came from the northwest. Their leader climbed the same mountain we were climbing, and when he came down . . ." she halted.

"Yes? When he came down?"

"Well, this is the part I misinterpreted. They said the man returned with some rocks that gave light."

My flabby old stomach tightened. Marisa saw the shocked look on my face and hurriedly continued.

"I know that's impossible, but I also know the word for "rock" and "light" and that's what they said."

"Lights from rocks?" I tried to look amused.

"Mom, I didn't hear them right, that's all. You know how these ancient myths explode into silliness."

"I've run into a few silly legends, myself." I didn't share my Cave of the Ancients experience. Maybe because I wasn't ready to explain something that unorthodox.

Next night, after dinner and clean up, the group sat around a fire pit, indulging in conversation. I encouraged Marisa to share her story, hoping someone had additional information.

"Is anybody here aware there's a sacred mountain a mile east of here?" she began. "The legend is that a ruler climbed up and when he came down he had sacred stones that gave light."

The young man sitting next to me stiffened. I felt it

like an electric shock passing through the air. His name was James and, according to his file, he was twenty-five years old and only on his first field assignment. I wondered what he'd done with his younger years when he should have been in school. He remained attentive but silent.

"Lights from rocks, huh," commented a young man who served as the squares supervisor. "How did ancient people come up with things like that? It's the wildest kind of story telling."

Dr. Bausch added his take. "It reminds me of poor old Percy Fawcett, who did explorations in Brazil during the 1920s. According to his reports, the Indians insisted they once had a special temple lighted by shining crystals. Fawcett died in the jungle searching for lighted stones and a lost city he called "Z."

"There must be a common thread that ties these myths together," someone else said through smoke and sparks. "But from Peru to China is a long way to look for threads."

"Or maybe from China to Peru," said James, almost to himself. This kid had an interest in the conversation beyond idle talk. Frankly, so did I. Shining stones were beginning to hound me, from bright globes in Tibetan caves to stones of light on a mountain in China, to illuminated ruins in Brazil. Percy Fawcett sounded like somebody I should know, but I'd never heard of him.

The topic around the fire moved to mundane things, like the politics of archaeology and how every dig is forced to generate income. Pure scholarship requires financial backing the way Da Vinci depended on rich nobility. We sang a chorus of *Money Makes the World Go 'Round* and fell into our cots, but my head still rang with the shining stones of Percy Fawcett.

CHAPTER 5

It rained. Cats, dogs, buckets, a wall of water. Average precipitation for the Shantung Peninsula is forty inches a year, and we must have gotten the whole allowance in half a day. Our dusty environment went from spatters on the tents to deep puddles at every entrance to leaks in the tent roofs. The pour was deafening, forcing us to yell at each other. Our tin-roofed kitchen sounded like a thousand monkeys with hammers pounding to get in. Everybody huddled in their private tents, and I was reminded of the deluge described in the Cave of the Ancients. It was probably like this, the day the sky fell.

Late afternoon saw black clouds dissolve and the surrounding countryside turn fresh and clean. However, our area, with all green life dug away, looked like a refugee war camp. Survivors met in the kitchen, wet hair stuck to faces, clothing disguised by mud. Dr. Bausch stood in line for hot food and I joined him. We'd developed a comfortable association, a kind of Old Boys' Club, and he'd consulted with me several times. Marisa and I were a valuable addition to his team. Marisa, poor child, had opted to stay in the soaking tent and eat Baby Ruth bars rather than rice, which she hated. She'd brought a suitcase full of chocolate, knowing she'd need some comfort food against a day like today.

The torrent had prevented meal preparation until the rain stopped, and we moved greedily for offerings of hot rice, noodles wound in individual piles, and the usual green weeds floating in golden oil. Sometimes meat was on the menu, but it hadn't been cooked that day, and only thin slices of fried Spam curled their burned edges on the platter.

"I can't get Percy Fawcett out of my mind," I said. "Could I pick your brain during . . . can we call this dinner?"

"Colonel Fawcett is an intriguing subject," Bausch smiled, "and I'd enjoy a chance to discuss him."

Dr. Bausch and I sloshed through dirty water to a corner table that the team on duty had cleaned. We settled in, Bausch put his round glasses on the table, and I gave him my rapt attention.

"He was called 'Fawcett the Dreamer' and 'Fawcett the Mystic' because he believed the fantastic legends in South America," Bausch said. "His work as a geographer was faultless, and if he hadn't ruined his reputation with hocus-pocus, he'd be counted among the great explorers of our age."

"You mentioned most of his work was in Brazil?"

Bausch swallowed hot tea from a tin cup, sucked in air to cool his mouth, and said, "Also Bolivia, four expeditions from 1908 to 1925. He believed he had the coordinates of a lost city he called 'Z', somewhere in Mato Grosso. He said the discovery would shift old notions of the world and change our knowledge of prehistory. On his final, fatal trip he took only his son and his son's friend, refusing to leave directions for a rescue team. He wrote that if he didn't survive, nobody could, and he didn't want to place anyone else in danger."

"Sounds like an unselfish man," I commented. Bausch had a piece of rice clinging to his graying mustache, but I wasn't about to tell him and break the spell.

"He was a genius and a nutcase," he said, "all rolled up into one nice guy."

I never understood men with mustaches, which would surely be itchy in summer and iced up from moist breath in winter. I tore my eyes from the rice bobbing up and down as Bausch chewed a limp weed.

"He believed there were lights from stones?"

"He called them 'lamps that never go out' and insisted a prehistoric civilization developed the technology. They were wiped out in a cataclysmic event."

I'd heard this before from Mahi, the Tibetan Monk in Thailand. But this was not the place for me to make a contribution. I wanted to encourage information.

"Ridiculous," I said. What else could I say? In my previous life of assuredness, an advanced technological civilization would have been "ridiculous." I finished with a statement patented by the scientific community:

"If such a civilization had ever existed, there'd be evidence."

"'Ridiculous' is what everybody said," Bausch nodded. "Fawcett would've done better and lived longer as an old Bible preacher."

I'd eaten my rice, noodles, tea, floating weeds, and even the spam while Bausch talked. I was finished and he was not. There's an unwritten eating rule that when the meal is over, the conversation is finished. Bad timing on my part. I scrambled to keep information flowing.

"He was a religious man, then?"

"His journal tells a story of a time he and his small team ran out of food and everyone sat under trees, waiting to die. Fawcett took his gun, crawled into a clearing, raised his arms as he turned east and west, and commanded food to appear. Fifteen minutes later a small deer walked by and the team was saved. Fawcett said the trick never failed but it had to be done with absolute faith."

"I'd say he was a religious man," I commented. "No wonder his reputation was tarnished in scientific circles." I came to the question that captivated me. "Did he actually see any of those lights he reported?"

Bausch reflected as he finished the last draught of tea in his cup. "He quoted the Echuca natives, followed them into jungles, looked for houses lighted with 'stars'—but never reported success."

I prodded a little. "Something must've happened to convince him the stories were true."

"Only the talk of savages." Bausch paused to chew spam, which, in my opinion, should be swallowed whole so the flavor stays away from the mouth. Finally he added, "Since the legends covered most of South America, Fawcett figured some truth must be there."

As an anthropologist, of course, I agreed. Ancient legends that cover an area the size of Brazil and Bolivia should be given attention. They usually have a particle of truth, though wrapped like a cocoon in shrouds of fiction. But I swallowed my comments and plied poor Bausch with additional questions.

"I'll bet you know more about this than you've said."

He grinned and wiped his mouth, catching the stray grain of rice. "Unending light sources weren't the only thing that got Fawcett in trouble," Bausch added. "He insisted that ancient people used a paste made from red leaves that dissolved solid rock. Massive stone monuments were melted, cut, and fused together with the paste, like mortar, then allowed to harden. That was his last nail in the coffin of acceptable science. Nobody listened to him again. Even his meticulous maps and journals were questioned."

"That must've been what kept him hunting," I interjected. "He needed proof to restore his besmirched character references." I took my chances with the next question. "Is there the smallest possibility that Fawcett was on to something?"

Bausch looked at me under thick eyebrows, then put his glasses on his puggish nose and began gathering dishes. "What do you think?"

Be careful, I warned myself. This may be a casual conversation now, but could strike you out later.

"I'm saddened at the thought of a man living and dying to touch a rainbow," I finally said.

The man sitting across from me, my official boss, leader of the expedition and fellow scientist, looked at the table as if something were carved on it. Then he quoted two famous lines from Henry David Thoreau.

"'The mass of men lead lives of quiet desperation . . . Live deep and suck out all the marrow of life.'" He looked up with an almost wistful smile. "Fawcett had rainbows he loved to chase. It was an enviable life."

That did it. I liked Dr. Bausch. Any man who can quote Thoreau and get emotional about it can't be all bad.

"Dr. Bausch," I said formally, a sign of ending, as we stood with dirty dishes on trays, "do you believe Percy Fawcett found anything?"

"Dr. Howard," he replied with equal formality,

straightening to his full height of five feet seven inches, "my official statement is 'no, I do not.'" He made a half turn and then faced me again to add another teaser. "But I can tell you that in 1947, a teacher named Hugh McCarthy from New Zealand traveled to Brazil, determined to find Fawcett's shining city. Hugh made a friend of a Priest at the edge of the wilderness and agreed to take seven homing pigeons with him, to let his friend know where he was. Only three arrived." Bausch paused to check the effect his story was having on me. I kept every muscle taut and didn't blink an eye. He appreciated my effort and continued. "One message said he had found Fawcett's city and he hoped the map had made it." I allowed a guttural sound to pass through my throat, something like "aarrrggghh," realizing that the pigeon with the map had not made it. Bausch kept going. "Hugh said he was dying, but it was worth it knowing his belief in Fawcett was not in vain."

I set my tray back on the table and bowed my head in frustration, only to raise it quickly when Bausch spoke again.

"By the way, did you know Alexander the Great had a glowing stone? He carried it in his belt as a talisman, but lost it on the shores of the Euphrates."

My face must have been a solid study of surprise because he laughed out loud at the sight of it.

"Aesculapius described it to the Emperor Augustus," he said. "Alexander's teacher, Aristotle, mentioned the stone, but the writing is lost now and can only be reported as legend. That's fairly recent history. You need to get your head out of ancient texts and join the present age." He winked and walked away.

What's in a wink? It means nothing and everything. It says "I'm joking" or "we have a secret between us" or "we can't speak of this again" or "you're all right for a fat old lady" or "I do indeed believe there are ancient shining stones." In my heart, I hoped his meaning was the last one.

C H A P T E R 6

"There's a find!"

The call came from the trenches. I was in a tent cataloguing the pitiful collection of potsherds we'd sifted from the gray clay yesterday. Earlier excavations had brought up bone tools, chipped stone implements, and animal teeth with holes bored in them for stringing into ornaments. A few fertility goddesses, which could have been toys, and six jade beads rounded out a respectable collection worthy of tourist trapping. A find now, fifteen feet from the present-day surface, was totally unexpected.

Everybody hurried down two levels of ladders to gather at the edge of a five-foot hole, defined by heavy string into a square. A grinning archaeology student, the girl who had unearthed the item, stood with trowel and brush, waiting for Bausch to lower himself in and identify the edge of chalky white protruding from a gray wall of dirt.

I could see from my vantage point that it was bone, flat like a shoulder blade, with scratches on it. Dark, methodical scratches like, oh, maybe writing. My bet was an oracle bone. Two thousand years ago, folks would write questions on bone, heat it up, and the breaks would indicate answers.

Nothing ever changes. Human nature demands answers to unexplained mysteries, like life and death, pain and sorrow, victory and defeat. If you play your cards right, the gods will tell you what to do with your life, the right decisions to make, whom to marry, how to get rich, how to be healthy, how to die at a very old age. Only the gods know, and you reach them by writing messages on the shoulder blades of cows. But this site was four thousand years old and shouldn't yield evidence of writing.

We watched as Bausch continued brushing, working the clumped dirt as if caressing a child's face with loving hands. It was indeed an oracle bone. What a shame nobody knew what the scratches meant. Not even Champollion could have figured it out.

"Well," Bausch said, "It's the same as twenty thousand other oracle bones in this area, but it shouldn't be this deep. Take the day off until tomorrow, when we'll be able to contact authorities."

A general cheer burst through the air and people scattered to make sightseeing plans or just lounge with a novel. James, the young man who had been next to me during the discussion of Percy Fawcett's shining rocks, walked over to Marisa and me as we stood at the edge of the rope-defined hole.

"I'd like to see that sacred mountain," he said.

"So would I," I agreed as I looked at Marisa. She was our ticket.

"Why not?" She found the Chinese men, spoke a few words, heads nodded, shook, nodded again, and they all returned. I figured this trip would cost a few coins.

"Let's go," she said. "They tell me today is a holy day

and we might have a lot of company."

The Communists had recently relaxed their anti-religion rules, perhaps because of the influence of western tourists. Hooray for the ping-pong politics of Richard Nixon. The horror of the "cultural revolution" was behind, and, for now, at this moment, we were going to see a sacred mountain with a history of shining stones.

The mountain loomed against the sky, its peak called T'ai Shan. It was beyond guessing how long the mountain had been revered, but emperors had been sacrificing at the top for more than 3,000 years. Someone built a grand staircase winding its way up passes and canyons, disappearing into chasms only to lift again with the next ridge.

From where I stood at the base, seven courses of stairway could be counted, following each elevation, broad enough to accommodate eight to ten people abreast. A safety wall on each side anchored the stairs to the mountain. I'd been expecting a simple, winding path, but it was majestic, in keeping with the finest skills and architecture China had to offer. This was a fortunate fact, since there were hundreds on the grand staircase, climbing slowly toward the summit. Our Chinese crew dissolved into the crowd.

"I'll take one step at a time," I said, "until I can't do another. Then you two are on your own."

"We'll help you all the way," James offered.

"At my age and weight," I countered, "you'll leave me alone when I tell you."

The ascent was steep, stairs close and shallow, and I kept to the right side, using the retaining wall for assistance. We tried to talk.

"James," I said, huffing up each shallow stair, "where's your interest in this? Architecture, ancient history, Chinese culture?"

"Personal," he said. "I have a book which tells about stones that give light."

"Really?" I tried not to sound anxious. "Light-giving stones are a newly-formed interest of mine. Did you know Alexander the Great had one?"

"Mom," Marisa lifted her eyebrow, a signal between us that I'd gone too far. The facial contortion was developed as a teenager when she realized I was unorthodox and embarrassing. She covered the signal by saying, "Are we going too fast for you?" but I knew it was a warning not to make up stories and call it history.

The fact is, I only tweak history a little to make it fascinating. One of my favorite quotes is from the play *Lettuce and Loveage*: "Fantasy floods in where fact leaves a vacuum." But I decided not to broach the subject of Alexander the Great because all I'd heard was the statement by Bausch. I'd hoped James might add something, since he knew about shining stones, but no evidence of recognition came from him.

I smiled and said to James, "What would I need to do to borrow your book?"

He grinned, but his smile was . . . wry is the word. A wry grin, crooked, distorted, while his eyes communicated that he knew something.

"All you have to do is promise to read it, the whole thing from start to finish. I won't tell you where the lighted stones are mentioned; you have to read 'til you find it."

It was a strange request, and my innards warned me of ulterior motives. But he was a good guy so I let the feeling slide.

"If there's one thing I do well, kiddo," I said, "it's read books. How do I get it?"

"I have it with me, but I'm taking it to the top."

I stopped midway between two steps. "You carry around a book about shining stones?"

"Yup. I always take it with me on trips."

James was pleasant but mysterious. He didn't quite fit in, but I couldn't identify anything wrong with him.

"Then I can borrow it tonight?"

"I'll bring it over to your tent when we're off this mountain."

On stair nine-hundred-sixty I lowered my old body to the hard, carved stone, announced my imminent heart attack, and told them to go on without me. Marisa opted to stay, saying she'd already been to the top. James appeared torn as he looked at us with concern, his eyes squinting against the two o'clock sun in the western sky. He looked longingly back at the mountain.

"I have to see this," he said as he turned to us. "When you're ready, go back to camp without me."

We protested.

He insisted.

"Please. I'd feel guilty if I thought you were waiting for me and . . . I really have to see this."

We struck the deal and watched him leave. Tall, slender, young, he could have taken two or three steps at a time and run up the course. But he set his eyes on the summit and took each step as if it were a religious experience.

"Interesting guy," I said to my daughter. "He knows more than he's telling. This place means something to him."

"Well, it means a lot of stairs to me," Marisa said, "and I can leave as soon as you want."

There we were, an old woman and a beautiful Chinese girl, dressed in decadent western clothes: t-shirts, Levis, sneakers, and baseball caps with beer logos on the front. Wizened, wrinkled old women stared as they passed us, and Marisa offered phrases of greeting. A few climbers stopped to chat. I'd listened before to the strange Mandarin melody explaining our presence in China, and turned my attention to other climbers who wore dun-colored uniforms and caps used by commoners. There were also polyester pants with flared legs, reminiscent of Sonny and Cher when they were an item in the sixties. Had those pants been imported thirty years ago? It was possible. Old-style polyester doesn't wear out, which is why western designers stopped using it. And now Chinese peasants would hand those pants down to their children. A thousand years from now archeologists could dig polyester pants from Chinese soil and decide they were used during obscure rituals. The stuff was obviously cold in winter, hot in summer, and couldn't possibly have been worn as clothing. They'd be wrong, of course. The ethnoanthropologist part of me enjoyed it when archaeologists were wrong.

We took the borrowed truck back to camp, leaving James and the Chinese guides to find another way. It was evening when the Chinese crew returned without James and told Marisa they'd left him wandering over various summits beyond the temple. They said not to worry. So, of course, we went to bed and worried.

The next morning I met James outside his tent, which was hardly bigger than a small pop-up, reflecting his status as a graduate student. Marisa and I were assigned a tent we could stand up in, no doubt the result of Marisa's value, not mine.

"James," I queried, "what on earth did you find on that mountain to keep you up there most of the night?"

"A little satisfaction," he replied.

"Did you learn anything that isn't in your book?"

"I learned the book is accurate, which I already knew." Then James randomly changed the subject. "Did you hear about the prehistoric burials found in Char Chan in the late eighties?"

"Yes, very interesting find," I said as I wondered what he was thinking. Why the switch from his book about lights to strange burials in China? I followed his lead. "They were Caucasian nomads dating four thousand years ago. Nobody knows what to make of them."

James anxiously added more information. "Some had traces of red hair, others were blond. What were they doing in China?" James was building up to something.

"All right, James," I said, "tell me what you're trying to say."

"Well, wouldn't it be interesting if they were crossing China on their way to somewhere else? Migrating to a new country, maybe searching for another home. They had domesticated horses and technology to make cooking pots. They weren't primitive. What if they could build ships and . . ." James trailed off. We were silent until I spoke again.

"Nice theory, James. Are you going to let me read your book?"

"Do you still want to read it?"

"Do I want to read it? You know, most people hand you a book and say 'here it is, have a good time, give it back when you're finished.' *You* act as if the book might be dangerous. What kind of book *is* it?"

He smiled, went inside his tent and brought back a small blue book, paperback, maybe five by seven inches, an inch and a half thick. Gold letters read "The Book of Mormon, Another Testament of Jesus Christ." I lowered myself into a canvas camp chair outside his tent and looked up at him.

"What is this?"

"It's my religion."

"Are you joking?"

"Truly, Dr. Howard, it's the most serious thing in my life. I'm a member of The Church of Jesus Christ of Latter-day Saints. 'The Mormon Church' is its nickname."

"James," I said, "I feel betrayed. You've used me to hawk your religion."

"I had no intention of . . ."

"I suppose you went on a mission, which is why you're behind in your education." It was a statement. I was familiar with Mormon missionaries. They'd knocked on my door a few times and I'd told them I didn't need religion.

"Two years in Dallas, Texas. The best, hottest place in the world."

"Do you have three wives and five kids at home?"

James lowered his head and shook it a little. But when he looked at me again it was with a sense of humor.

"One wife, one kid, another coming."

"Well, James, it isn't nice to fool little old ladies on archaeology digs."

"I'm not fooling," he said. "There really is a section that talks about lights from stones. It's surrounded by faith in God, but . . . hey, you asked me for it."

"It's not real. I'm looking for bona fide, certifiable lights from stones. Not some Mormon mumbo-jumbo about faith."

James was visibly hurt. His eyes dulled a little as he clutched the blue book. My acid tongue had lashed out and spread poison. I smiled to soften the blow, but I refused to do a full backstroke.

"Look, James, I'm from Arizona where Mormons think they own the state. Your people are everywhere. Newspapers defame you. If Mormons run for office, it becomes a campaign issue and nobody votes for them. Do you want to know what we called you when we were kids?"

"You've got my attention," he said.

"You guys are 'the Church of Cheese and Rice of Rattle-day Snakes.'"

"What?"

I'd gone too far again. I shouldn't have shared that old joke, but it was too late.

"The Church of Cheese and Rice of Rattle-day Snakes."

James stared for a split second, then threw his head back and laughed a great, bellowing howl.

"That's the funniest thing I've ever heard," he gasped. "I gotta remember that." He practiced the name a few times. I helped him. The tension dissolved.

"Dr. Howard," James finally finished, "you asked to read this book. Accept it as a gift from me. It spent most of the night on top of T'ai Shan and can serve you as a memento of this trip. If you never get around to reading it, it'll still look good on your bookshelf next to the Bhagavad Gita, the I Ching, the Torah, whatever you have."

"I have all those books, and I haven't read them, either," I said.

"All the same, they stand as examples of your broad-mindedness. I hereby release you from your promise to read my book. But if you ever get curious and take a peek inside, my name and address are printed there and I'd like to know what you think. We part as friends." He held the book out to me.

"I consider the promise null and void in any case," I grinned as I took the small volume, "since it was made under false assumptions. But I accept the book as a memory of you and this trip. We do, indeed, part as friends."

I took the book to my tent, placing it on the table between our cots. When Marisa saw it that night she lifted her eyes to the canvas ceiling.

"So *that's* what all the cryptic nonsense was about."

"He's a nice kid, Marisa. It's a gift."

"You don't really intend to read it, do you?"

"I have a lot of strange books in my library," I said. "I collect them. I don't believe them."

Marisa shook her head in friendly disgust. "Whatever," she said.

Discovery of the oracle bone brought Chinese authorities to the site. Marisa and official government interpreters kept busy with the faults and foibles of communication. Nobody knew how to explain the bone, which should not have been there, full of Neolithic writing that should not have been invented yet. It was decided to be an anomaly, buried during a much later time for reasons no one could imagine, even though earth disturbance was lacking. Why would somebody living thirty-five hundred years ago bury their oracle bone beneath a prehistoric site? Probably to cause trouble later. They must have died laughing.

CHAPTER 7

We left China with its misplaced oracle bone and said our good-byes to friends and colleagues. When I came to Dr. Bausch, he took both my vein-riddled hands to squeeze.

"You and Marisa were a definite addition to my team."

"You know," I said, "it was pretty obvious you had to take me in order to get Marisa."

"That's true," he said. "But now, both of you are welcome at my digs anytime." We laughed at the old-fashioned play on words. 'Digs' could mean a house as well as a literal archaeology dig. If Marisa had been there, she wouldn't have gotten it.

"Matt," he said, "keep looking for lights."

I grinned and moved on.

James gave me a hug.

"I think you'll like my book, if you ever get around to reading it," he said. "Remember, write and let me know what you think."

"What if I think the whole thing is hogwash?" I asked.

"I still want to know," he cheerfully answered.

Marisa and I hugged at the L.A. airport, promising we'd do another adventure. I watched her elegant black hair swing across her shoulders as she moved toward the Chicago terminal. Three hours later I collapsed in my own bed, grinning at the ceiling, glad to have gone and grateful to be home. It doesn't get better than that.

Unpacking was quick, since I've learned to travel light, and the little blue Book of Mormon was placed next to a large volume of the *Bhagavad Gita*, a Hindu scripture I'd picked up in India. I stood back and cocked my head sideways to see the titles of the two volumes leaning against each other. I decided to arrange them on their backs so the spines could be read easier, with the smaller Book of Mormon laid jauntily on top of the *Gita*. Nice touch. It looked like I might even be reading them. Perhaps, when I was old and senile, I'd take one down and actually look inside.

A week later when I cleaned up my field journal, I found the notes about Percy Fawcett with a reminder to read his journal, *Lost Trails, Lost Cities*. I phoned the university's massive library and they promised to have the book ready to take home when I got there. Ah, the privileges of membership in the ivory tower. Professorship has its moments of advantage.

Fawcett's book was a small four-by-six hard copy with age spots on the cover—or maybe they were gravy stains. Someone had underlined parts and written in the margins, which I appreciated. It helped in skimming the contents. The story could have been a script for an Indiana Jones movie: pure adventure filled with eighty-foot anacondas, hostile savages, voodoo, and massive cities from an unknown civilization destroyed by cataclysmic earthquakes. It featured human atrocities, slavery, murder, and disease. I played with the notion of re-writing Fawcett and selling it to Hollywood under my own name.

Naaah, I thought. Dr. Bausch would rat on me.

I took Fawcett's book to my desk, intending to make notes from its pages. Early in the book he told of a red leaf used by Incas to soften rock for easier carving. The report was written as if taken for granted, with no more importance than a boundary coordinate. I found the episode Bausch had related, when Fawcett commanded food to appear: *I did what I had never known to fail when the need was sufficiently pronounced, and that is to pray audibly for food. Not kneeling, but turning east and west, I called for assistance, forcing myself to* know *that assistance would be forthcoming. In this way did I pray, and within fifteen minutes a deer showed itself in a clearing 300 yards away.*

Bausch was right. Fawcett should have been an old-time Bible evangelist, preaching faith, prayer, and knowing.

Shining stones were mentioned toward the end:

Pg. 234, *The Indians there spoke of houses with 'stars to light them, which never went out.' This was the first but not the last time I heard of these permanent lights found occasionally in the ancient houses built by that forgotten civilization of old.*

Pg. 298, *The point where we leave civilization is described by the Indians as a sort of fat tower of stone. They are thoroughly scared of it because they say at night a light shines from door and windows! I suspect this to be the 'Light that Never Goes Out.' Another reason for their fear of it is that it stands in the territory of the troglodyte Morcegos, the people who live in pits . . . .*

Pg. 299, *My rancher friend told me he brought to Cuyaba an Indian of a remote and difficult tribe, and took him into the big churches here thinking he would be impressed. 'This is nothing!' he said. 'Where I live, but some distance to travel, are buildings greater, loftier, and finer than this. They too have great doors and windows, and in the middle is a tall pillar bearing a large crystal whose light illuminates the interior and dazzles the eyes!*

Fawcett's final statement was as Bausch had described it:

Pg. 315, *If we should not come out I don't want rescue parties to come in looking for us. It's too risky. If with all my experience we can't make it, there's not much hope for others. That's one reason why I'm not telling exactly where we're going. Whether we get through and emerge again, or leave our bones to rot in there, one thing's certain: The answer to the enigma of ancient South America . . . and perhaps of the prehistoric world . . . may be found when those old cities are located and opened up to scientific research. That the cities exist, I know.*

There was that "knowing" stuff again. How can you "know" anything without seeing it? Without touching, tasting, hearing, smelling it? I lose patience with people who "know" things they can't possibly know. Fawcett sacrificed himself, his son, and a friend because he thought there was a city in the jungles of Brazil. Did he see his oldest son die and blame himself? Did he think of his family in England? What motivates a man like that? Pure stupidity?

The energy of anger had me searching my house for something to dissipate the feeling. I stood at wall-sized shelves scanning colorful book jackets until I noticed two books, face down, spines easy to read. I grabbed the blue one on top, The Book of Mormon.

A plush chair next to my library collection distributed the weight of my backside, a hand lever raised my tired feet into the air, and I opened the cover of the book I'd planned to read twenty years in the future. The flyleaf contained a message from James to the world at large: "This book belongs to James Marchant. If found, do not return. Keep it. Read it. Tell me what you think." There followed an address and phone number. Good psychology.

I always look at the flyleaf, publisher, copyright dates, dedication, foreword, and introduction, to see if a book is worth my time. Books don't write themselves. Somebody is always responsible: an ordinary human with problems, quirks, frustrations, axes to grind, and points to prove. Books, like the people who write them, need to be evaluated before rushing into a long-term relationship.

Behind the front cover of The Book of Mormon I learned that Mormon was the ancient man who compiled it. Joseph Smith translated and published it in 1830. There were intriguing terms on the flyleaf: people of Nephi, Lamanites, Moroni, Book of Ether, and Jared. The one-page introduction explained that the book revealed two great civilizations in the Americas, and included an appearance by Jesus Christ. Smith's own three-page story told of Moroni, now an angel, who led him to a hill where the plates were buried.

I leaned my head into the soft cushion of my favorite chair and wheezed a groan. If somebody wrote a book like this today, no respected company would publish it. If the author paid to self-publish, the bookstores would file it under "fiction." Smith chose the only time in history when his book could emerge. I turned my attention back to Smith's story.

After four years of instruction from Moroni, Smith got the plates, two interpreters called Urim and Thummim, and translated the book. Then he gave the gold plates back to the angel. I turned the page and . . .

The phone rang. I snapped the book closed, set it

on the side table, pulled the lever to lower my feet, and pushed my bulk from the cushions. I loved being in that chair. It was getting out that I hated.

The phone was on its last ring when I grabbed it. The phone company gives me three rings and then jumps to my message machine. I can't move fast enough to get anywhere in three rings, but I keep forgetting to ask how to increase the time. I hit my knee getting to the phone.

"What." I was grumpy.

"Dr. Howard?" a man's voice. A surprised man.

"Yes, this is Dr. Howard." I regretted my rudeness.

"Matt? This is John."

Well, of course it was John. He held keys to the doors I wanted open, so he would naturally call when I was grouchy and rude. The script of my life had been written by an enemy.

"I wasn't sure it was you, Matt," he said. "You didn't sound like yourself when you first answered."

"Sure I did," I laughed. "I sounded like myself when I'm irritated." After a comment like that I felt I owed John an explanation so he wouldn't take it personally. "I'm reading The Book of Mormon. What do you know about Joseph Smith?"

"Don't tell me you're getting sucked into . . ."

"No, no, I'm angry about Percy Fawcett and started reading Smith to get over it, but now I'm interested in Smith."

"Who's Percy Fawcett?"

"He's a dead man. What do you know about Smith?"

"He's a dead man, too. He wrote The Book of Mormon and got killed. Beyond that, the only thing I know is a joke."

"I'm ready."

"Mormons are like giant mayflies. They look scary, chase after lights, and make a nuisance of themselves . . . but they don't bite."

I'd heard the joke before, but laughed anyway.

"Well, John, I'm glad you called. Can you get me to Brazil?" It was an off-the-cuff remark, prompted by the recent reading of Fawcett's journal. I had no idea the impact that innocent statement would have.

There was a short silence.

"What are you up to, Matt? How do you know about Brazil?"

My brain did a fast-forward to inform me that if John thought I had secret information, it placed me in a position of power. I'd better keep it that way.

"Well, you know me, John," I said breezily. "I keep my ears open and things fall into them."

"Who told you?"

"Now, John," I said, "I shouldn't disclose my sources." I needed to keep that upper hand. "Pretend the regular channels haven't been breached and tell me what you called about." I had accidentally fallen into something big.

"I assume you know it's in Mato Grosso," he said.

"Naturally," I lied. I was good at it.

"Since you already know," John said, "you may as well also know I called three specialists before you."

"That's very flattering, John."

He ignored my sarcasm. "I didn't give them details, since the find can't be made public. They weren't interested in a jungle dig, even though Dave Johnson is heading it up. Johnson finally suggested you, but I told him I didn't think the assignment was right for a woman, much less an old . . ." he caught himself.

"But Johnson disagreed," I spoke quickly, "and wanted . . ." *Think! Think! Mato Grosso, a state in South Brazil; wild jungle; the natives would be very primitive so the team wouldn't need an ethnoarchaeologist.* I took a chance and completed my sentence, " . . . a pottery specialist."

I heard John's vocal cords tighten as he spoke. I knew it was happening because his voice got higher. "I can't believe somebody would talk to you and not let me know." *Bingo,* I thought. *They need a pottery specialist.* John continued. "It's a jungle out there, Matt, and that's not a joke. It isn't safe."

"Yeah, yeah, I know. Eighty-foot anacondas. Will you be going?"

"Of course. I can't miss something like this. The pottery looks Sumerian, and it doesn't seem possible that . . ."

"Wait a minute," I cut in. "Did you say 'Sumerian'?" I couldn't believe what I'd heard.

I could almost see John grin, his gold incisor peeking from the corner. "Sort of gives you a clue how important the place is, huh. They can't bring samples out for thermoluminescense or fission track dating, so they need someone with real expertise in Middle Eastern pottery."

"I guess that's me," I said. whatever they'd found couldn't leave the site, which was a clue to something unusual. Sumerian artifacts in the jungles of Brazil? This was more than exciting; it was earthshaking, even scholar-shaking.

"I know I'm not the first choice," I said, as a safe statement, "but tell Johnson I'm on the team. When do we leave?"

"I'd hoped to move on to someone else." John was ever so candid. "But since you already know about it . . . as soon as possible, within the month. We'll meet the team in

Brasilia. Get your affairs in order, your insurance paid up, and your relatives informed. I still think it's a bad . . ."

"You can't scare me off, John. Send the itinerary."

Sumer, the great creator civilization in Mesopotamia, had predated Babylon, Assyria, and even Egypt. The Sumerian golden age lasted from 5,000 to 2,000 BCE when it disappeared into the sand to become a mere myth. In the late 1870s, a French diplomat in Iraq got bored with his job, dug up some sand dunes, and found the advanced culture. And now it shows up in Brazil?

I couldn't plan a trip I knew nothing about, so I went to a movie . . . a fantasy adventure in which an eighty-foot anaconda swallowed everybody on the boat.

CHAPTER 8

The flight from Phoenix to Washington, D.C., was four hours. I spent the time rehearsing ways to tell John I knew nothing about the project. The words typed themselves inside my head.

John, you're gonna laugh when I tell you how I accidentally misled you about . . .

No good.

Look, I need to level with you. When I said 'could you get me to Brazil' it was a fluke . . .

Huh-uh, it wouldn't fly.

John, I know you didn't want me to come, so I'm feeling a little guilty about . . .

There was no way to tell him I needed information. John already felt betrayed thinking someone had informed me without his permission. If he found out I'd lied, even innocently . . . all right, it wasn't innocent . . . I'd pay a heavy price. He had the power to ruin my career, not to mention my reputation. For some reason a quote from my childhood Methodist Sunday School days surfaced: "Sufficient unto the day is the evil thereof." I didn't know what it meant in its Bible context, but for the current situation it was a reminder that my little treachery would be discovered sooner or later. I decided to make it later. By the time the plane landed in D.C., I was ready to dance around the issue until I figured it out on my own.

The next leg of the trip, D.C. to Brasilia, was nine and a half hours, plenty of time for twenty questions.

"You know, John, I'm curious why pottery sherds can't be brought back for testing."

"Didn't your informant tell you?" John was still miffed.

"My informant didn't tell me anything important," I smiled amiably. "In fact, you'd be surprised what I don't know."

John looked sideways and lifted one eyebrow at me. The gesture said he didn't believe me, but he'd be civil and answer the question anyway.

"Brazilian authorities aren't completely informed on what's been found," he said. "Anything taken from the site could cause an unpleasant incident."

"I can see that," I said.

"Even worse," John looked ahead, as if talking to someone superimposed on the back of the chair in front of him, "if word leaks out to the press, it'll be Roswell in media-land."

I took the cue. Roswell, New Mexico, was still controversial as the supposed crash site of an alien spaceship fifty years ago. Media coverage caused a War-of-the-Worlds reaction.

"Right," I said. "TV documentaries would hint at alien transplants from Sumer to Brazil." I checked John's body language to make sure I was on safe ground. It looked good. He picked up the narrative.

"More than just hint," he said. "It doesn't help that the Nazca Plains are right next door in Peru."

Okay . . . the Nazca Plains . . . Peru . . . animal figures carved on miles of flat desert ground. A best selling book claimed the area was an ancient spaceport because the figures can only be seen from the air.

"I agree," I said, nodding my head. "And Brazil is second only to the USA for UFO sightings." How did we get to alien spacecraft from a find in Brazil that tied to ancient Sumer?

"That's all we need," he said. "More talk about the lines of Nazca used as space airports."

I added my two bits to keep the ball rolling. "That whole Nazca Plains thing was cleared up as a hoax," I said, "when it was pointed out that the figures weren't large enough for small airplanes, much less spacecraft."

"But the damage is done," John said. "Late night TV still airs the *Mystery of the Nazca Lines* every time they have a couple of hours to fill."

"Uh-huh," I quickly agreed. John had experienced some bad press during a dig in Egypt and didn't trust the media. His graduate student had claimed the Sphinx was five thousand years older than currently believed, and the press involved John's name. Unofficial talk about visitors from space surfaced, since no one believed that prehistoric earthmen could have built the Sphinx. That incident explained why John was sensitive to anything that smacked of weird science.

"After the entertainment people finish with the find in Brazil," he went on, "legitimate scientific funding will go right down the drain."

"You're speaking from experience," I said. "I remember what they did to you in Egypt." I hoped I was still entering the conversation appropriately.

"If they get to it first," John said, "we won't have a

chance at supplying a logical explanation."

I took a deep breath and asked John a pointed question leading to a few facts I could use.

"What's your impression of the find?"

John pulled his left ear, an act I'd seen him do many times during the thirty years I'd known him. Translated, it meant he would deign to speak his opinion.

"The description resembles a lost city reported by a Portuguese team hunting for treasure mines in the 1750s. The staircase passage is a dead giveaway. I'm sure you've heard of it."

Hello? A staircase passage? Keep going, keep going.

"No," I said, "This is all new information. I always learn something valuable from you. Please continue." A little one-downmanship seemed wise at this point. John took the bait.

"Dave says guano is mid-calf and higher, so the place is old, maybe 3,000 BCE. They use masks to avoid guano inhalation while they're in the ruins."

Score two points. The city had been reported in the 1750s and is large enough to make bats comfortable. The place sounded as old as anything in Mesopotamia. I nodded to encourage John to keep talking. He did.

"Apparently, the report was sent to the viceroy at Rio de Janeiro but ended up in government pigeonholes for the next two hundred years. It's barely legible now, but Johnson knows a villager who showed him the passage."

"The staircase passage?"

"Right."

"Where would Dr. Johnson find someone who knew the way?"

"Dave was in Brazil delivering medical supplies to a village. A grateful shaman offered to show him where the 'ancients' once lived."

"And how does the shaman feel about us trooping in to see a sacred place?"

"That's why everything is secret and the team is small," John said. "Dave doesn't want to betray the shaman's trust. We're not looking for gold or treasure. We're looking for history."

"John," I said, "that is profound. Thank you for letting me come." The statement was sincere.

John closed his eyes and shook his head.

"Matt," he said, "it's a mistake . . ."

"Don't start," I interrupted. "It's too late to change things. I'm here and I'm glad. Thank you."

We had seven hours to read, doze, sleep, dream, and snore. I did the snoring.

In Brasilia, Brazil, David Johnson met us at baggage and shook my hand.

"Pleasure to meet you, Dr. Howard," he said. "We've already uncovered some exciting things and are glad for your help. I assume John's filled you in on everything."

John spoke quickly. "She's been informed."

"I'm missing details," I said. "It'll be good to get the whole story from you. And call me Matt."

Johnson was in his forties, a skinny six-foot-tall man topped with bushy brown hair that needed a shampoo and cut. His eyes appeared too large behind glasses held together at the bridge with surgical tape. I liked him immediately. It was the surgical tape that did it. Obviously, Johnson wasn't aware of himself, his importance, or his image.

"I prefer to be called Dave," he said. "The rest of the team are picking up supplies in the city and snake serum from the poison center."

Ahhh, yes. Snake serum to match the snakes we'd be

stepping on. We pushed our way from the baggage claim to a van and stacked our bumpy duffle bags to the roof. The three of us squeezed in the front seat and drove to the *Centro de Controle de Intoxicacoes de Brasilia,* the Poison Center, where Dave introduced the rest of the team: three more men and one woman, all in various degrees of being thirty to fifty years old. They were grizzled and burned, skin peeling from noses, hair matted, fingers bandaged . . .and smiling. The prospects of a hot bath, dinner in town, a good sleep, and an early start in the morning must have seemed heavenly. Two women and five men made a good ratio for balancing professional opinions. I greeted the woman heartily, not only for her expertise, but also because I figured her presence guaranteed a civilized outhouse arrangement.

The surprise was a short, squat little man, maybe four and a half feet tall, with shoulder-length black hair and a Mayan hawk nose. His chocolate skin was deeply wrinkled, with eyes so dark they seemed eternal. Dressed in loose, dirt-caked white pajamas with a rainbow serape slung over one shoulder, he stood out from the rest of the group like bright color on a black-and-white photo.

Dave introduced the tiny man as "Pop," our jungle guide who could get us to and from the mystery site. I smiled and nodded. He returned a barely perceptible sideways movement of his head, but his dark eyes could read me. I squirmed under his gaze and was relieved when Dave began a conversation with Pop that took attention away from me. He used a simple sign language, punctuated by staccato sounds which Pop returned. The anthropologist part of me whispered that here was a unique individual. I determined to learn the hand signs and interview Pop as soon as possible.

"Snake serum is just a precaution," Dave said as we toured the poison center. "The daily danger is mosquitoes, and we battle them with everything we've got. You have all the shots, I hope. This isn't a good place to get Dengue Fever. It might not kill you, but you'll wish it would."

I collapsed that night in the hotel without knowing, or caring, what the others were doing. There'd be time enough for socializing during work at the site. The next morning the eight of us molded ourselves in three vans, using spaces not filled by supplies, and headed out the back streets of Brasilia to the jungle. Five hours of teeth-jarring, bone-rattling travel later, we parked and locked the vans in a newly cut clearing and began transferring supplies to individual backpacks.

"How much farther?" I asked, to no one in particular.

"We'll hike until dark, then make camp," Dave answered. "Tomorrow, it'll be another four hours to the passage, three hours inside, and two hours to the city."

The passage took three hours? I swallowed my surprise and nodded as if he'd just made a normal, logical statement. Dave gave me a concerned look.

"I don't want you to get exhausted," he said. "We need your professional experience in the field and I've arranged for Miguel to carry your pack on the supply wagon. All you have to do is keep walking."

"Well, Dave, you warm an old woman's heart," I said. "I know my limits. Thank you for the kindness."

No good was served by false pride. I was sixty years old and overweight. Maybe I could carry personal items, but my share of the camp supplies would be an impossible load on senior shoulders. The last thing I wanted was to slow down the trek.

I gave my backpack to the young man identified as Miguel, a graduate student of David's. He seemed a trifle testy, like an angry teenager who believes he's being taken advantage of. Perhaps he thought David had brought him along as a packhorse. I wondered if he knew how fortunate he was to be part of this adventure at this time and place. He wore a ragged T-shirt that said *there are two theories to arguing with a woman . . . neither works.* I thought it was funny and said so, but he only grunted as he took my pack and tied it on the wagon. Miguel was obviously not impressed with an elderly woman's long list of credentials. "Thank you," I said. He ignored the gratitude, probably thinking he'd be hauling me on the wagon before the day was over. I determined to prove him wrong, hoping my lifetime routine of yoga and a daily walk would finally prove itself worthwhile.

A second, heavier wagon was handled by two other men, and additional items were parceled out among the rest of the team. I was embarrassed that I couldn't carry my share and apologized. Everyone was gracious. John and Miguel were silent on the matter. I couldn't blame them. John wanted me gone and Miguel was carrying my load. We lined up single file behind Pop and stepped into the forest to follow an invisible trail, trusting our lives to the strange little man with piercing eyes.

The jungle folded over us.

CHAPTER 9

I've slept in trains, planes, and buses; curled up on concrete roofs in India; and breathed the hot night air of a Thailand tree house. So sleeping in a hammock strung above ground in a Brazilian jungle should have posed no problem. Pop helped me choose the right trees so creatures couldn't crawl along the ropes, burrow under my skin, and lay eggs. That alone should have brought an easy slumber, but I had the distinct impression something watched me.

The jungle shrieked with cries of living things, all of them looking for a snack. About the time I dozed off, something brushed the underside of my hammock. To my credit I didn't scream, but I stayed stiff the rest of the night, like a child waiting for the closet door to squeak open. I expected the next sensation to be jaws clamped over my head.

Morning was barely perceptible under the canopy of leaves and vines. Only a filtered version of the sun made its way through. We'd slept in our clothes, so cleanup was quick. Hammocks and mosquito suits were rolled into packs, Pop did his usual sweep for poisonous things so we could answer nature, and we were gone. No need

for hair coiffing or eyelash curling—or even a change of
underwear. It was a forced march by consensus, everyone
anxious to get to base camp.

An hour's trudge later we stopped for a break in a
clearing. Protein bars that tasted like a ninety-nine-cent
variety of sawdust were handed around. My attention
wandered to a group of birds on a rocky escarpment
twenty feet away. They fluttered into round holes in the
side of the cliff, but the holes didn't look natural. They
were too neatly formed, nicely circular. I took another
bite of protein bar, stood from my folding campstool, and
began walking toward the cliff to get a closer look. A
small brown hand placed itself on my arm. It was Pop.

"Hello, Pop," I said, looking down and smiling.
Children were the only people shorter than me, and I had
to remind myself that Pop was an adult. I used gestures to
communicate interest in the nests. Holding my right arm
perpendicular, I formed a circle with the fingers of my
left hand and placed them against my arm. "What makes
the holes?" I pointed to the cliff and began walking.
Pop stopped me again, shook his head and looked at the
ground four feet away.

Straining to identify what he was seeing, I noticed a
slight movement among the stalks. My eyes widened and
the skin on my scalp tingled as I realized there was a large
green snake in the grass.

"Thanks, Pop," I said.

He nodded, picked up a stick, and cleared a space on
the ground to draw a bird with a leaf in its beak. Then he
pointed to the actual cliff where a living bird clung like a
woodpecker, rubbing a dark reddish leaf over the rock in a
circular motion. I noticed other birds pecking at the cliff,
burrowing in, and kicking out red leaves with leftover

pebbles. It was as if the solid rock had turned to wet clay.

"Well, I'll be . . ." I laughed aloud. It was Percy Fawcett's red leaf in action, the leaf used to soften rock, cut it precisely, and fit it to the next megalith. Not even a thin knife blade could be slipped between the cracks. Primeval man must have watched these birds, the size of a kingfisher, and figured out applications for the red leaf. So, Percy Fawcett's story was fact. Maybe the city with shining stones was also true.

I called to the group, who were still murmuring about the chalky protein bars.

"Hey, somebody, come take a look!"

"What have you found?" It was David.

"You've got to see it before you'll believe it!" I felt pressure on my arm. Pop looked at me and shook his head, his black eyes commanding. This little man had a power larger than his size.

"Have you found something worth getting up for?" It was the other female archeologist, Shirley. I liked her. She laughed with genuine joy at the smallest excuse.

"Naw," I replied. "Pop was showing me a snake in the grass." Pop had his reasons for keeping the red leaf a secret, so I let it die there . . . the secret, not the snake.

We left the dense jungle to travel through bush country where an hour's hike brought us to our first glimpse of a jagged mountain range at the other end of a grassy plain. These were not ordinary mountains. The sides lit up in flames, streams leaped from rock to rock, and a rainbow formed through the mist. The peaks looked like gemstones piled by a giant hand.

John stood next to me, absorbing the sight. "It's exactly the way they described it," he said.

"They? Meaning the Portuguese treasure hunters?"

He nodded. "They thought the mountains held the mines they'd been seeking. When they got closer they realized the sun reflected light from sheet crystal and opaque quartz. Hardly great treasure."

"Well, it looks like diamonds from here," I said.

John stared at the mountains and spoke as if he'd memorized the old Portuguese report. "All day they struggled over boulders and crevices, trying to find a way up those glassy sides. Rattlesnakes were everywhere, and they finally decided to give up."

"Thank you for that piece of information about rattlesnakes," I said. He ignored me.

"They set up camp for the night. Two guys went looking for firewood, startled a deer in the brush, and chased it. They lost it beyond a cliff, but the men found a shaft going up through the mountain and saw daylight at the top."

"The staircase," I said.

"The staircase," he repeated. "If they'd been searching for the passage they never would have found it. They had to stumble into it." John was silent as we both stared at the rugged range.

"What are the chances of stumbling into a hidden passage through that mountain?" I asked.

"Oh, about zero," he replied. "That's why we're the first to see this place in two hundred fifty years. Whoever lived on the other side of those mountains was safe from enemies as long as the staircase could be defended."

David joined us, doubling his long body into a crouch and resting his arms across his bony knees. "That's quite a view, isn't it," he said. "In three hours we'll be climbing through the passage. I've been here three times and still can't find it without Pop." David paused a moment. "He's nervous about the size of the group."

"The size?" I said. "There's only eight of us. That's an unusually small team."

"Pop showed me the ruins as a personal favor," David explained. "He wasn't planning a group tour. He's been looking around like he expects lightning to strike any minute."

I tried to add a positive comment to pick up the mood. "I think Pop knows we're not looking for treasure. He'll be all right."

"Our object is to get history . . ." John started to say. It was the beginning of a famous quote from Sir Leonard Wooley, spoken at the ruins of the Sumerian city of Ur. It was one of my favorite quotes, so I picked up the sentence and finished it for John, " . . . not to fill museum cases with miscellaneous curios." I knew as soon as the words hit the air that I'd made another mistake. John should have been allowed to finish the quote. I have a voice inside that tells me when I've been stupid after the fact, but no voice to stop me before the deed is done. Someday I'll complain to my programmer.

David didn't seem to notice the tension. "We may only be after the truth, but Pop's nervous."

Three hours and two aching feet later, I stopped to put moleskin on baked blisters. I'd worn the steel-toed, high top boots suggested as protection against jungle critters, but now I longed to kick off my miserable toe dungeons and run barefoot in the grass. I said as much to Shirley, who hiked in front of me.

"You don't ever run barefoot in the grass here," she laughed. "In fact, you don't run at all. Movement is slow and easy, so you don't scare the domestic denizens. By the way, you're gonna continue sleeping in those shoes, you know."

The hope that she was kidding must have leaked out through my face because Shirley touched my arm to say quite seriously, "It's better than waking up some morning with stumps for feet because something gnawed your toes off during the night."

I shut up and kept trudging. Eventually I began a parody of *The House that Jack Built*: " . . . This is the smudge that Shirley left, who stepped in the blotch where John once tramped, who plodded the trail where David marched, who followed footprints that Pop had left, who scanned the grass for beasties while leading us to the ruins." I repeated the poem over and over, gradually adding the three men behind me. It was a great way to learn their names until, finally, I didn't care about their names. Boredom will do that to you. After a while, I stopped thinking.

The mountain seemed to fall in our collective lap, almost as if the thing had moved to meet us and intended harm. Steep, slippery, sneaky in the way it placed its boulders, the behemoth was designed to prevent crossing. We tripped, stumbled, slid, grasped hands for support, and followed Pop. Occasionally, someone would yell a warning about snakes or rolling rocks. The rocks presented more immediate danger.

Suddenly, Pop vanished.

I stood still, shocked as I watched David turn right and merge into the cliff, followed by John. Shirley faced me, grinning, and slowly melted into the solid rock. First her left hand disappeared, then the arm, shoulder, laughing head and backpack, until only a right hand beckoned and waved its dramatic exit. When it was my turn to face right, I entered a dark crevice that immediately broadened until I faced an upward curving path, exactly like a staircase.

The four hikers ahead of me were already climbing up and passing from view behind the wall that braced the curving route. I walked forward and looked up. We were in a chimney so tall that light flowing from the top spent itself long before it could reach the floor. I craned my neck to see a pinpoint so far above me that it looked like a large star. The movement put me off balance. I reached for stability against the walls, touching both sides with the span of my arms, and felt something furry against my left hand. Reaction was electric as I pulled away. Peering closer, I recognized a growth of mold or lichen and realized a diffuse light made it possible to see, as if illumination came from inside the walls.

It did.

Everything was studded with crystals, lighting my surroundings like a half moon on a dark night. Here was the fairyland I'd created in my mind as a child, with magic sparks and astral mysteries. It was so beautiful I had to remind myself to breathe.

A command shattered the enchantment. "Don't use your flashlight! Pass that on." It was David. I repeated the words and heard them quoted like an echo behind me.

"Why not use flashlights?" I had to ask.

"We'll be climbing this shaft for three hours," he called back. "It's safer to develop night vision."

Good-bye, fairyland.

The chimney was a down-on-its-luck spiral staircase, most of it deteriorated to dust, but still rising on a sculpted incline. As my vision improved, I noticed chisel marks on the walls. This passage was man-made, enlarged from a natural fissure.

The first hour of our climb was fascinating. I touched

cool, damp walls, examined lichen, and exulted in faint fairy-light reflected from the top of the chimney by clear crystals and quartz. I studied the quartz, knowing it was an opaque rock and had to be carefully faceted to catch the light. The angles were diamond-sharp, of excellent workmanship, and they'd been embedded in the walls by the hand of man, tool markings surrounding the placement. It was phenomenal. Then I stopped caring.

The second hour of endurance brought oppression, the noise of exertion, and smell of sweat. The three men below me wrestled with equipment wagons, heaving, shouting, joking, and swearing. Their personal packs had been portioned throughout the group, but their effort was immense and I felt guilty that my pack was part of their burden. Nothing could be transferred at this point. The spiral moved up, like a dysfunctional elevator, and we were committed to move with it.

The third hour brought diabolical proof of the hate the mountain held for us. Air was hot and moist, carrying the smell of decay. The ancient stairs crumbled and slipped under my exhausted old body. Shirley finally tied a rope under my arms and handed one frayed end over John's shoulder. Together they gripped the line across their overburdened backs and kept me upright. I was past embarrassment, concentrating on survival.

Lift one foot . . . pull the other foot up . . . rest and breathe . . . start over. Lift one foot . . . pull the other foot up . . . rest and breathe . . .start over. A miniscule voice at the center of my medulla whispered that someday I'd have to travel back through this nightmare of a hole. I told the voice I wouldn't do it. They'd have to hurl me down the chasm like a human sacrifice.

The walls seemed to move in on me, pressing against

my lungs, burying me alive. I knew they were still an arm's length away, but I was hallucinating and needed all my energy to fight panic.

Suddenly a strong tug on my leash brought me to my knees and I fell onto something flat, pebbles peppering my cheek. Several hands lifted me and guided me a few steps.

"Hey, you made it. Welcome home." It was a gentle voice from another world. Then came words that were not so gentle.

"C'mon, Matt. Open your eyes and look at this sight." It was my affable enemy, John. Were my eyes closed? I willed them open, commanded them to see, but they loitered in darkness before focusing.

We were in divine open air on a substantial ledge, high above the surrounding plain, big enough for all of us to rest on. Sounds of the men still struggling with their loads in the chimney blended with bird songs carried up the mountain from the forest floor below. Those who still had stamina moved back toward the passage to give aid. As for me, I lowered myself into the dirt and, with legs stretched out, acknowledged gratitude to someone in the universe, someone I didn't know but needed to thank. The ordeal was over. We had climbed the passage and emerged on the backside of Neverland.

And then I saw it. Perhaps four miles away, situated on the banks of a shining river, spread in all directions with spires and pyramids and temples . . . a testimony of an ancient, glorious past. The entrance gate appeared massive, even from this bird's-eye view.

It was the lost city.

CHAPTER 10

M att, where are you?"
"I'm still up here."

"What are you doing?"

"I'm looking." The mountain ridge stretched as far as I could see, from southeast to northwest, and in the distant north lay hazy, unbroken forest. The foreground was a sizeable plain, dotted with trees and dappled in places by shining pools of water.

David's voice lifted to find me. I'd once floated in a hot air balloon where the racket of children, dogs, and lawnmowers rose like heat to my ears. It's funny how sound drifts up.

"Matt, get down here with the rest of us. Stop dawdling!"

"Right!"

I hurried to catch the group descending a hundred yards away. We followed a rocky trail down the mountain and across the plain. A few hours later it brought us under three massive arches, the entrance to the city, formed of blocks weighing at least fifty tons each. It resembled the fortress of Sacsayhuaman, Peru.

"Our technology can't do this today," I said to the

world at large. David heard the statement and stopped. I continued. "Our cranes couldn't lift fifty-ton rocks into a three-story gate like this."

"We'd use rebar and concrete and make a pretty fair imitation," David said, "but we couldn't build the real thing."

We passed through the center arch to a wide street littered with broken pillars and carved masonry. I put a cramp in my neck trying to take it all in. Houses, two stories high, lined the avenue, built of great blocks fitted together with joins of incredible accuracy. I moved for a closer look and then stopped and opened my penknife to see if the blade could be fitted between the . . .

"Matt! What are you doing!" It was John this time.

"I'm dawdling."

"Well, cut it out!"

"What's the hurry?" I asked.

David answered. "We need to be in the tents before dusk."

"What happens at dusk?" I stood where I was, next to the two-story house, my penknife open. I couldn't bring myself to rush through this city. It would be like running the Grand Canyon River with my nose in a novel.

The answer came in chuckles and sniggers, a joke at my expense. Even John was in on it. Obviously, the price for lagging behind was missed opportunities for show and tell. My emerging blisters sneered at me through thick pads of moleskin as I limped toward the group, wondering what happened at dusk.

A collection of comments by the team held my interest.

"Look at the massive stone slabs that form vaulted ceilings. These people had modern tastes."

"Modern tastes but not modern technology. How did they get those chunks of rock up there?"

"There's examples of corbelling, too. Beautiful work. Like precise stone steps in reverse to support an arch. There's something for everybody in this city."

"Have you determined engineering differences in construction? I see some buildings are almost whole, while adjoining ones are demolished." John asked the question. He was no dummy. It was a shame we didn't trust each other.

"Construction seems uniform. The weakness might be connected to the soil. Later, we're planning to chart the entire city and plot destruction to see if there's a pattern."

I looked at derelict balconies and imagined faces peering from ruined windows. The wasted skill of these ancient builders grieved me. People should still be here, joking, gathering water, gossiping in the street, chasing naughty children. I longed to peek inside the roofed structures, but the acrid smell of bat dung assaulted my sinuses. Immediate exploration lost its charm.

A half mile later the broad way opened to a vast square, a third the size of a football field, four obelisks of black stone standing in each corner. At the center of the square, on a column of the same black material as the obelisks, stood the effigy of a man, one hand on his hip and the other pointing north. The statue was too tall to see detailed facial features, but it appeared perfectly preserved.

"Has anybody examined this guy's face?" I asked.

"Not yet," Shirley answered. "We're starting from the ground and working our way up. When you see what we've found, you'll understand why 'Napoleon' here is down the list." She waved her hand at the perfect specimen of a vanished race, then turned to inspect her tent for anything dangerous that might have moved in during her absence.

The team's base camp had been set up months earlier on the square's stone paving, which offered a solid foundation for specimen tables, tents, and kitchen facilities. It was also a safe choice, the clearing was free of vines and tangles for creatures to hide in. I knew I should set up my tent, but housekeeping chores were down the list. Unbelievable evidence of an advanced civilization beckoned. The team must have found something spectacular to ignore a central showpiece like the man pointing north. I climbed on his ebony pedestal, clung to his thigh, and searched where he directed.

Beyond the square, the north part of the city lay in total ruin. Edifices were buried under mounds of earth on which not a blade of grass or other vegetation grew. Here and there were gaping chasms where whole buildings had been swallowed, only corners peeking from their graves. There was little doubt what had devastated the place. I'd seen evidence of massive earthquakes before. A few short minutes of a devastating cataclysm had erased the work of generations of men.

"Is the view good up there?" The man who spoke was Doc, one of the men who had pulled the wagons. His real name was Travis, but they called him "Doc" after the dwarf in Disney's *Snow White*. He fit the part, short and heavyset, in his late forties, with a coarse, gray beard. Glasses perched on his red nose to complete the Disney impersonation. During the ordeal in the chimney, he'd gasped and wheezed, expressing positive hope he'd be fifteen pounds smaller once he reached the top. It lightened the moment.

"Hey, Doc," I said. "The view tells me this place had

an earthquake. I've got a question."

"We dragged you here hoping *you'd* have answers," he shot back.

"Fooled ya'," I said. "Why hasn't the jungle covered that place? Why doesn't even grass grow in those north ruins?"

Doc ran a hand through his thinning hair. "There are cracks over there so deep that when we dropped rocks down, we never heard them hit bottom. We explored the area our first week here and came back with roaring headaches, so we think a poison seeps up and contaminates the air. Nothing lives in it. When we've finished this side of the city, we'll get oxygen equipment and do a study. Meantime . . ."

"Meantime," I said, "the grass is not always greener on the other side."

Doc helped me slide down and I wandered west where a magnificent building ran the entire length of the plaza. The walls and roof had collapsed in places, but square columns still stood, and a broad flight of steps led into a wide hall. Even from the plaza I could see traces of color on frescoes. Over the main portal stood the carved figure of a beardless youth, head crowned in a wreath, shield in hand, a band across one shoulder. Writing was inscribed above, not Greek but resembling Greek.

Ramiro moved next to me. I didn't know him well, since he, Doc, and Miguel had pulled the wagon while I staggered ahead. He was young, in his thirties, five feet eight inches, with light brown curls around his face and neck. Built like a short Arnold Schwarzenegger, it was obvious why his assignment was the supply wagon. He put those rippling muscles to good use. I nodded at the carved soldier over the door with writing underneath.

"Looks Greek to me," I said, tongue-in-cheek.

"The Portuguese thought it was Greek in their report," Ramiro said, "but it isn't. The script might be Greek Linear A. I know it's impossible, but there it is."

Examples of Linear A had been found on Crete and the mainland of Greece, but no one had deciphered it.

"It's a shame the folks who carved this didn't use Linear B." I said. "Didn't some guy decipher B in the 1950s?"

"His name was Ventris, an architect who worked on Linear B as a hobby in his spare time. Guys like that give professionals a bad name."

I laughed. "Amateurs have all the luck. By the time professionals get to the field, the clues have been destroyed. That's why this place is so amazing. We're the first."

"We're fortunate the Portuguese never made it back here," he said. "They were after treasure and would have razed this place. Now, it's pristine." He blew a kiss to the young man wearing a wreath.

"If Linear A is what we're really seeing," I said, looking at the carved script above the door, "pinning this place to something definite isn't going to be easy. It would be nice to know what these people had to say."

Ramiro shook his curly head. "The key word is 'if.' If it's Linear A, the fact that both A and B are found on Crete could give us a handle on a date. The Minoan civilization hit its peak about 3000 BC, but this script doesn't look familiar. It could be a modified version of A or something we've never seen before. For now, we're going with the 3000 BC figure."

Ramiro had said BC, meaning "before Christ," instead of the politically correct BCE, meaning "before the common era." It told me something about him, but I wasn't sure what. Was he a religious man? Or did he just like to rebel against political correctness?

"Maybe the flow wasn't from Greece to Brazil," I said, chancing a reputation for perverseness. "What if this is a prehistoric civilization that exported Linear A to Crete six thousand years ago?" I'm an old woman. I can say outrageous things and be forgiven.

Ramiro didn't even flinch at the suggestion that civilization could have moved from west to east.

"Right now, nothing would surprise me," he said. "This place will take decades of research, probably past our lifetimes." After a moment in quiet contemplation of our own mortality, Ramiro changed the subject.

"Have you seen the building on the other side yet?"

I turned to face the ruin of another huge edifice across the plaza, not a twin but a complement. If the first was a government structure, the second was a palace. Eroded carvings of animals and birds covered the walls that remained, and over the portal were more Greek-looking characters. A movement inside the halls caught my attention. Small black creatures circled through dim chambers. I looked closer.

Bats were stirring. Thousands of them.

"We'll need to be in our tents before dusk," Ramiro said. "You don't want to be caught without shelter when those guys come out to play. Tomorrow is time enough to catch up on the splendors of the city."

He helped me pound tent pins deep into the dirt between paving slabs and I organized my favorite things: my cot with extra reinforcement so it doesn't sag in the middle; an aluminum folding table with pen and paper on top in case a brilliant idea comes in some forgotten moment of the night; three cardboard drawers to hold the necessities of life; and, the final touch, four small laminated quotations taped randomly inside my tent. One of them could always reach me at the right moment and make me laugh:

I used to have a handle on life, but it broke.

Quoting one is plagiarism; quoting many is research.

The gene pool could use a little chlorine.

And my favorite:

I have a degree in liberal arts. Do you want fries with that?

I looked around the finished tent. I was home.

At dusk, the mouth of hell opened. I'd been to the famous bat caves of Thailand, but that was kindergarten; this amounted to a world-class vampire metropolis as countless bats left their lofts in the city to feed in fields beyond the river. It was Hitchcock's movie *The Birds*, a black nightmare of frenzy, screams in decibels so high my ears only registered pain. Sheer numbers forced some to fly low and a few leather wings hit the tent roof. I hid next to the cot, arms over my head, expecting a rat with wings to tear through the canvas. In five minutes the hysteria ended and peace filled the night, accented only by a howler monkey impersonating a large feline. Or it might have been a large feline.

I slept with my shoes on.

CHAPTER II

Morning brought good news: no dead bat bodies littered the plaza, so nobody had to sweep them up. I sauntered to the mess tent where Doc and John arranged breakfast items on an aluminum table.

"I volunteered to remove dead bats today," I said, "but it looks like I'm out of a job."

Ramiro helped himself to oatmeal. "You'll make up for it tonight," he joked. "You and I have the dinner assignment. I'll meet you here at five, and I hope you can cook."

"Sorry, Ramiro," I said. "The green thumb I don't have for gardening shows up in the kitchen. People turn green when they eat my cooking. But if you can give directions, I'll try and follow."

"The group is in trouble," he said.

I noticed David sitting at a table slurping a carton of orange juice. I walked over and slid into the bent aluminum camp chair across from him.

"So far," I said, "I've seen architecture that looks like pre-historic monuments in Peru and writing that might be Greek Linear A. When do I see Sumerian pottery?"

"As leader of this expedition," he smiled, "I insist you

eat first, because once you set eyes on the collection, you won't want to leave the tent."

"That good, huh."

"We'll bring you a protein bar for lunch because I guarantee you won't be thinking about food."

I moved to the food line-up, slopped oatmeal into a bowl, checked the raisins for legs before scattering them on top, and poured reconstituted powdered milk over the whole mess. A quarter cup of brown sugar made it edible, and I retraced my steps toward the table where Ramiro and David were having a serious discussion. Ramiro was doing the talking.

"It's a light toward the northeast. I'd guess it's on top of a pole or a tower because it shines above the forest and doesn't move. It never goes out."

"Ram, there's nothing out there. No cities, towns, villages, nothing to produce electricity."

"I know what I've seen." Ramiro sounded determined. "I've taken some readings and I'd like to check it out."

"If you can wait until tonight, I'd prefer to see it, too, and then we can plan."

"Fair enough."

Ramiro stood when he saw me. "Hey, Dr. Howard, I wish I could be there when you see what's in the big tent." Actually, "tent" was a grandiose name for several large pieces of canvas thrown over a frame.

David also rose to leave. "Most of the artifacts you'll see today came from building twenty-seven in section one. The roof is still intact, so the treasure hasn't been crushed. We can thank Miguel for the find. He was willing to dig through bat dung to uncover those babies."

"Thanks to him," Ramiro said wryly, "we all have to muck through the stuff now, just in case there's another cache of treasure."

David patted Ramiro on the back, like a dad giving encouragement to his little leaguer, as he said to me, "We'll be interested in your professional opinion after dinner."

The pressure was on. I'd published a book about pottery twenty years ago. It was so boring that it still held an honored place as required reading for unfortunate undergraduate students. But the focus of my thoughts at that moment was Ramiro's sighting of a constant light in the distance. I was haunted by Percy Fawcett, who claimed a large tower served as a boundary marker for the city he called Z . . . the city he died trying to find. Both tower and city contained lights that never burned out.

I promised myself I'd be out that night to see the light in the forest. In the meantime, there was a twelve by twelve foot "tent" in the square that was calling my name. In fact, I realized, it was literally calling me, inside my head. I heard it like a thought that wasn't mine.

Come.

"You're getting old, sweetheart," I said to myself. "Now you're hearing things." I remembered a statement written on one of my T-shirts: *You're just jealous because the voices only talk to me.* Maybe it wasn't a joke and this was the first step to insanity. *Come*, the word insisted, intruding into my brain again. I shook my head and started toward the artifact tent.

There were four tables, three loaded with bundles wrapped in muslin like drab Christmas presents. Pop stood at the end of the first table, unwrapping items and setting them carefully in place. The team had covered and tied each article for safekeeping while they were gone to Brasilia. Now Pop was preparing the items for my inspection.

"Hello, Pop." Should he be here, handling this

valuable collection? How could I tell him to leave? He smiled when he saw me and pointed to the opposite end of table number one, with the clear meaning that I needed to start my work there. He acted as if he were in charge and I held a position as his assistant. Lack of communication made it easier to just play along, but I intended to watch him for clumsiness. What was David thinking? I would certainly have a talk with him this evening about the wisdom of . . .

Suddenly, Pop wasn't my focus. The first item on the table was a bone mask staring up at me through narrow slanted eyes that reached to the sides of an elongated face without ears. The nose extended from the top of a peaked head to an equally sharp chin. There was no mouth. It resembled the face of an alien in a grade B science fiction movie. I'd seen a similar mask on the other side of the world, but this one was bigger. I wondered what kind of animal was large enough to provide sufficient bone from which to carve this thing.

Look. Words in my head again. I squeezed my eyes and rubbed my forehead, then noticed Pop in front of me, the cataloguing notebook in his outstretched hands. I took the book.

"Did you say something?" I said. I knew Pop didn't speak English, Spanish, or Portuguese, but there was no doubt I'd heard words. He turned, businesslike, back to the second table where he carefully unwound a three-foot-tall alabaster vase. I moved closer to examine the intricate carvings, which included human figures marching around the center panel. Pop looked at me, raised his eyebrows, and nodded at the first table. Had he just ordered me back to work? Incredulous, I realized I didn't dare defy the little pipsqueak and slunk back to my assignment. I sat on the only chair in the tent and paged through the notebook filled with sketches of the artifacts. When I found the drawing of the stylized bone mask, I entered the words *Sumerian, Ubaid Period, 5900–4000* BCE. After checking to make sure Pop wasn't watching, I quietly flipped through the notebook to the vase, now sitting in reality beyond my reach on table number two. I furtively wrote: *typical of the Uruk Period, 4000–3000* BCE. I felt like a kid at school cheating on a test, hoping the teacher wouldn't catch me.

The treasures on table one snatched my attention and sucked me in. I didn't notice when Pop finished his task and left. Occasionally I drank from a water jug, and I was vaguely aware that someone brought two protein bars with several drink cartons. I swallowed the wretched things without tasting them, complete awareness concentrated on the table. Black and red paints, human figures, geometric designs, and curved spouts were all reminiscent of early Mesopotamian finds. Pottery showed evidence of production on a fast turning wheel, fired in kilns. There were plenty of potsherds to sacrifice for positive dating later, but I'd seen enough to know that the results would match early Sumerian dates. I didn't know how to explain it. "Anomaly" wasn't going to do the job. It took seven hours to examine and catalogue the first table.

At five o'clock Ramiro began meal preparation. I opened, cut, chopped, and scrambled ingredients for a stir-fry over the small propane stove.

"Ramiro, I heard you say you saw lights in the forest."

"I *thought* I saw a light, just one light, but it was a long way off. I'm sort of embarrassed you heard me. You'll think I'm nuts."

"When you go out tonight with David, would you kick on my tent flap so I can see the light, too?"

"Do you believe me?"

"I'll go one better, Ramiro. I know you saw it and I think I know what it is."

Ramiro smiled like a child who had just received major adult approval. "Expect that kick tonight," he promised.

After dinner, the group discussed table one and I confirmed the Sumerian connection.

"We need to date clay samples in this area and do a comparison study against the pottery," I said. "If they were made in Mesopotamia and brought here, we have some mysteries to solve: How did those traders get to this city on the other side of the world? What trade goods did they take back, and have we assumed everything found in Sumer is Sumerian when some of it could be from Brazil? How can we separate the two civilizations? The second possibility is more formidable: if manufacture is local, the design similarity to Sumer can't be coincidence. There's a missing link, an advanced people we've lost. Everything we know about the beginning of civilization will have to be rewritten."

"We'll be starting a new section of the city tomorrow," David announced. "Maybe we'll find things specific to this culture and be able to distinguish between this and Sumerian."

Miguel spoke, something he rarely did. "Maybe building number twenty-seven was a kind of museum where they kept items from Sumeria, and daily use articles will be found somewhere else."

"Whatever we find," David added, "We can expect more surprises."

"Do me a favor," I said. "Keep Pop busy so I can run

a quick preview of the other tables. He thinks it's his job to keep me on task, and I feel compelled to obey him. It's embarrassing."

David laughed and assured me Pop would be doing something else. I glanced at Ramiro, whose face was lost in a grin, and realized the two men planned to take Pop with them when they searched for the light in the trees. David was convinced it existed, even without the night's planned preview.

"Ramiro," I warned, "don't forget your promise." I had to see the light. He nodded.

That night I sat on my cot and waited for the bat feeding frenzy. Then I patiently listened for the expected kick at my tent. I wrote in my journal, cleaned under my fingernails, turned out the light, and waited. My head nodded into my clavicles and, still sitting upright, I entered a zone of doze.

Bump.

One kick? That's all I got? It was a good thing I hadn't actually been asleep. I jerked up and stumbled into the night. There was no moon, which was fortunate, since a moon might diminish the light we expected to see. Still, the stars were overwhelming, obnoxious in their brilliant, swirling patterns.

Three figures walked ahead of me, one the size of a child. Pop was there. I quickly caught up.

"Hi, guys," I whispered. "I wanna come, too."

"What are you doing here?" David asked. He wasn't angry, but maybe a little annoyed. Ramiro hadn't told him I was coming.

"I know what this thing is," I said.

"We haven't even seen it yet, how can you know?"

"There's this book by Percy Fawcett about . . ."

"Let's see it first, then analyze." David was grouchy, probably sleep-deprived. Or maybe he didn't like people crashing his parties.

We moved across the plaza in silence. Ramiro led us past the northeast corner and down a wide street for a block or so. A slender pyramid rose thirty feet to greet the stars, with stairs so steep it required all fours to climb. David and Ramiro were in the lead, I came next, and Pop was last. It was a rugged climb. Stairs were becoming the curse of my old age.

"Ramiro," David said, "what were you doing up here in the middle of the night?"

"I saw the light the first week we were here," Ramiro answered, "and thought it might be an atmospheric shift. But I saw it every night and finally scouted out this pyramid during the day to get a better view."

"Answer the question. Why were you out here? It isn't safe; you know that."

"I've got a small bladder. What can I say?"

When we reached the top, bent over and gasping, the platform turned four people into a crowd. Why did those ancient folks go to all the trouble to build a thirty-foot pyramid with no room on top? Maybe it once held the neighborhood satellite dish.

"There it is." Ramiro pointed. "It's always there, every night, peeking just above the trees. See it?"

You can't judge the distance of a pinpoint of light. I squinted, then refocused. It was solid, not twinkling or moving, steady as a halogen lamp.

"All right, Matt." David turned to me. "What is it?"

"Colonel Fawcett's tower," I kept my eyes on the bright spot.

"Whose what?"

I told the story, Fawcett's explorations, his journals, the report of a tower with a light. "It marks the area boundary of a city he said would transform history when he found it," I said.

"Maybe the city we're in right now is the place Fawcett was looking for." Ramiro sounded hopeful and I hated to tarnish his theory. But I did anyway.

"Fawcett said his city had crystal lights and was close to a large waterfall. Our place was discovered by the Portuguese and doesn't answer the description of Fawcett's dream city."

David was all business. "Obviously, Fawcett never found his crystal city or we'd know about it."

"Obviously," I agreed. "He disappeared before he could make a final report."

Ramiro was like a little boy looking for answers. "What's the light made of?" he asked. I decided to give him both barrels.

"It was manufactured by a technologically advanced prehistoric civilization, using inert radioactive chemicals infused into crystals. The process took nine years under intense heat. There's a cave in Tibet still lighted by the globes. It's full of ancient machinery and a story of worldwide destruction, and there are similar repositories in Egypt, Peru, and Siberia. There could be others. Alexander the Great carried one of the shining stones with him, but . . ." I caught a glimpse of the looks I was getting from the two scientists. I didn't need bright moonlight to know what they were thinking.

"C'mon, Matt. Where are you getting this stuff?" David now saw Dr. Howard and Ms. Hyde for the first time. "It sounds like bad science fiction." I couldn't blame him. This was way beyond acceptability, verging on cock and bull.

"I'm not going to validate Percy Fawcett's journals," I said, "but you can see the light for yourself. What do you make of it?"

After that, David and Ramiro ignored me. They discussed how far the light might be and took additional readings. David and Pop exchanged clicking, guttural sounds, fluttering hand signals in the glow of starlight. It was easy to tell what Pop was saying. He was adamant about not going. The same word, repeated several times, was undoubtedly a resounding "no," and David's word was probably "why not?" Pop lost patience, said his word one more time, then turned and climbed down the pyramid.

"He says no," David explained to Ramiro, even though the explanation was obvious.

"Can we go by ourselves?" Ramiro asked.

"No."

"Why not?"

"It isn't safe."

"Then we need Pop."

"He says no."

"Can I go?" I interrupted before thinking. The timing was perfect for the reaction I got, two male voices in unison:

"No!"

"Oh, well," I replied.

I'm persistent to a fault, hanging on like a Gila monster when necessary, but it was quitting time. I take pride in knowing when to give up.

I would soon be grateful for that character trait.

CHAPTER 12

Angry voices outside my tent uttered clicks and guttural sounds. I entered the early morning light to see Ramiro with two backpacks at his feet, which he kicked at softly as David and Pop uttered their strange language. He avoided eye contact with his teammates, who watched the tall, slender man and the child-sized brown one spar linguistically. I didn't need to know the language to guess the interpretation, since gestures and facial expressions are universal. The conversation probably went something like this:

Pop: I will not lead you.

David: We just need to know what to expect, what's out there. You don't have to go.

Pop: You cannot go. You will die, even with your guns.

David: We must go.

Pop: Why do you search for that which is forbidden?

David: It's our nature.

Pop: Your nature is foolishness. I have brought you where danger is high. To go further is death.

David: We'll go, with or without you.

David turned from Pop and looked at Ramiro. "C'mon, Ram. It's time to head out." Then to the group, "Carry on, folks. Business as usual. Ram and I have some checking to do and ought to be back tomorrow."

"Tomorrow when?" It was Doc. "If you don't come back after a certain time, do we go in after you? Judging by Pop's reaction, maybe we should all go and . . ."

"We'll be back. Don't come after us." Then to me, "Matt, you can fill them in." The two men struggled into heavy packs and headed to the northeast corner of the plaza.

Pop sat on his haunches and rolled himself into a tight ball, hands covering his face. He rocked back and forth, emitting soft moans. As the sound increased I realized he was chanting a prayer of despondency. We watched Pop perform his ritual, which lasted perhaps a minute, ending in sudden stillness. He looked like a round chocolate ball in a colorful wrapper. Slowly Pop unfolded himself, picked up his small bag and primitive bow, and walked across the plaza to join the two men who had disappeared down the skinny pyramid street. We watched until he was out of sight. Doc turned to me.

"All right, Matt. Let's hear it."

I told them about the light Ramiro had seen and the trek last night with Pop. I didn't mention Fawcett's journals or his search for prehistoric cities with eternal lights. There didn't seem a good point in introducing fanciful distractions. No one had anything to add, so Doc, the second in command, ordered everyone back to work.

The artifact tent felt lonely. Items on the tables didn't beckon the way they had yesterday, their swathings now limp and ragged. I sat in my wretched, wobbly chair to begin cataloguing a magnificent inlaid game board, hollowed out to hold its carved playing pieces. There was a vase made of electrum, the kind found in Sumerian graves. I uncovered a handful of small, decorative clay cones with painted floral motifs at one end. They would have been driven into pillars to make colorful designs. The pillars would be somewhere in the city and I should have been excited, but I couldn't concentrate. There was an uncomfortable fact, lost or forgotten, hidden in a niche of my brain, almost there but not there. I discarded the shapeless thought and picked up the fourth item on table three, an ornate woman's headdress with tall flowers of gold sprouting from the crown. Leaves and vines encircled what would have been the woman's ears when she wore the hat. I imagined how the Portuguese explorers might have celebrated if they'd found this headdress. It was only a cash commodity to them; they would have melted it down for the gold alone, like savages who can't understand the value of a computer.

I remembered. The source of my elusive discomfort hit me.

Fawcett had said no one could get close to the lighted tower because of savages who lived in underground pits. They couldn't be seen until they attacked. There would be no signs of habitation; no huts, no fires, no clues. I should have told David. I should have warned him. They were walking into a trap. Pop knew. That's why he chanted his song before he joined them.

I sat at my table of extraordinary treasures and wrung my hands.

It was a long day and a long dinner. The silence was too loud for conversation and we avoided each other's eyes, hoping not to see the collective concern. Words were utilitarian.

"Pass the salt?"

"Sure."

"Did we ever get ketchup in town?"

"I think Ramiro got a bottle." An uncomfortable shifting of chairs, then a weak, "But I don't know where it is now."

Doc stood and broke the barrier. "After the bats tonight, I'm going out to see this light. Does anyone want to come?" A general murmur of agreement followed. "Can you lead us, Matt?"

At ten that night the five of us balanced on the skinny pyramid platform, linking elbows to prevent anyone from falling.

"What's a light doing out there?" Shirley stood on her tiptoes to get a view. John answered in his usual gruff manner.

"It's a star coming over the horizon. If we wait awhile, we'll see the change in position."

"Which star." Miguel didn't ask normal questions; his tone sounded like a challenge.

"I don't know which one!" John's voice squeaked higher, which I knew from past experience indicated frustration. "I'm not an astronomer. Use your heads, folks! There's no light out there. It's in the tops of the trees; ergo, it's a star on the horizon."

Doc was gentle when he spoke. "I can't see David and Ram making a mistake like that. Did Pop know what the light is?"

"You saw how Pop acted this morning," Shirley said. "That wasn't just a song in the plaza. It was a prayer. Whatever the light is, he's afraid of it."

I listened without talking, which was not my default mode, but a growing dread had moved into fear; genuine, primal fear. Three men out in the jungle were in danger, and the five people balanced on this pyramid platform weren't much better off. Not one of us knew where we were or how to get out. The thought crushed the air out of my lungs.

"We've seen it," John finally said, breaking the silence. "Let's go."

Morning was slow coming, breakfast was slow eating, the day's assignments were a slow routine. At 12:30 we met in the mess tent to prepare lunch when Miguel walked in and casually announced, "They're entering the plaza."

We couldn't get out there fast enough, running to meet them, cheers of victory, questions rudely jumbled into each other like reporters at a press conference.

"Man, are we glad to see you!" Doc smiled from one rosy cheek to the other. "It's been a regular funeral wake here the last twenty-four hours." The smile faded when he saw David's face. There were two of them, David and Pop, moving at close to a run. Sweat mottled their smudged faces. We hurried to keep their pace.

"Everybody, listen up," David was grim. "We're leaving. Take only your backpacks, a little food and water, mosquito suits . . ."

"What about the equipment?"

"We're leaving everything but survival gear. Move it, people, there's no time to explain."

"I don't see Ram," Miguel said. "Should I go help him?"

"He doesn't need help."

"Wait a minute. Where's Ram?"

"Get your pack, Miguel."

Miguel stopped moving. "Where's Ramiro?"

"Ram's dead." David kept moving.

The five of us stopped next to Miguel for three seconds of cold, stunned silence. Then, as if we'd had an electric probe, the group ran to catch up to David again.

"What do you mean, dead?" It was Doc.

"I mean dead!" David stopped and held his head in his hand for a second, then said quietly, "Dead. Now move." We ran with him, hearing his backpack bouncing and jingling on his shoulders.

"I need information," Shirley said, panting, trying to keep up. "Where's the body? How did he die? We can't leave him there."

"The jungle has carved up the body and carted it off by now." David's voice rose, part anger, part grief. "Do you think I would have left him if there'd been any other way?" His jaw was tight as he added, "No more talk. We have to get out of here."

I entered my little domain, slowly reviewed what I'd need, and pushed items into my pack. The world turned from color to black and white, then moved to slow motion. It wasn't possible, the death of my curly-headed, muscle-bound young man, bright and funny, with a long life ahead . . . I felt a presence, turned quickly, and faced Pop. I could see the pattern of sweat on his face, then realized it wasn't sweat, but tears. He stared into my eyes and I heard desperate words inside my head, as clearly as if they'd reached my ears: *Tell everyone to run! Now!*

The little man's alarm terrified me and forced me into action. I held my pack in my arms rather than take time to fit it on my back, rushed outside and yelled as commanded. "We've got to run! Now! Don't stop to get anything. Run!" My panic roused them to action. Shirley joined me as we headed for the boulevard that led to the main gate. Doc came close behind, and David and Miguel caught up. John stood still. The stupid man would never move on my authority.

"NOW, John!" David shouted behind him, and John took off at a gentle jog. The group soon left me behind. My fight or flight reflex was still operational, but the mechanics were faulty. I looked back to see Pop staring across the plaza, then a single word in my head, *Run!* So, it was not my imagination. Pop used telepathy.

I was aware of the massive gate around and above me as we exited the city, three arches made of cut stone so large a modern crane couldn't lift it. Pop moved next to me with his thought-words, *They come.* I vaguely wondered how he did that, and how my brain could translate, or if the whole communication was a matter of human emotion and whether . . . then somebody who looked like Miguel took my pack from my arms and sprinted ahead, bringing me mentally back to this lost city in the jungle of Brazil where we were running for our lives. Pop remained with me, encouraging me along the trail and up to the mountain where I'd first seen the city, just four days ago. I wasn't sure if we'd spent hours or minutes getting to the platform. The soil still held my imprint from when I'd collapsed out of the staircase and expressed gratitude to some unknown god. It seemed strange to see evidence of my former existence when my present time was not part of reality. The others were already in the chimney, rocks and pebbles rolling inside, proof of their hurried presence.

Go, came the word in my head. *I stay to protect. Tell David good-bye. I feel sorrow.*

I looked down at the view, the pristine ancient city, the pyramids, temples, homes, and saw a quick shifting through the trees. A bush shivered, a shadow slipped behind a rock. I never actually saw anybody before Pop pushed me down the hole. I missed the first thirty steps and bumped into John.

"You okay, Matt?"

"We're being followed! Move faster!" I said the words but it wasn't my voice. It was too high and too loud. As an afterthought I added, "Thanks for asking."

We focused on our uncontrolled slip down the chimney full of crumbled steps to the other side of the mountain, where we continued sliding to its base. John moved ahead and David came back to check on me.

"Where's Pop?"

It was the moment for truth, and I hated to be the bearer of it.

"Pop stayed behind to protect the staircase."

David's tall body leaned into a boulder and he lowered himself carefully, hand over hand to the ground, as if he had become a very old man. I sat on the boulder, grateful for a moment of rest. He stared across the savannah for a second, then words tumbled, some out of order, but they couldn't be stopped.

"They came out of the ground," David said, "like the special effects of a bad movie, they lifted themselves up out of the dirt. Ram saw the tower first and wouldn't stay with Pop, he didn't listen, he didn't see any danger. No huts, no fires, nothing, just a tower with a magic light in it. When he moved into the clearing there was a quiet "phoosh" sound, then several more, like people breathing. Ram fell to the ground with little darts in his neck but it wasn't real to me. I stood there searching for the source of the sound while Ram twitched and died in the clearing. I don't remember when we started running, but Pop cried all the way, running and crying, running and crying."

A gunshot startled us. John was ahead, looking at something in the tall grass. "I'll bet he just killed a snake," I said. I'd been on the verge of telling David I'd known about the primitive tribe that guarded the tower. No good could come from that piece of information so I stood, the cue for David to rise, and we began a rapid walk to catch the group.

"Pop said good-bye," I told David. "And he said he was sorry."

"How do you know what he said?" David spoke mechanically, like a trained scientist. He didn't look at me. I assessed the situation and decided David was too exhausted, physically and emotionally, to hear about Pop's telepathic ability. Furthermore, I didn't want to be placed in the center of another Twilight Zone episode. Apparently Pop didn't communicate telepathically with David, and I was too weary to field questions. I gave him the easiest answer.

"I watched you talking and figured a few things out."

"He's dead, too," David said. "What have I done?"

My own guilt was so heavy I had to shake my head to stay focused. A physical sickness rose from my gut to my heart. Two good men were dead because I hadn't warned David about the danger at the tower. It was too late to prevent the tragedy, and it wasn't my place to give mothering, reassurance, or confession. All I could do was listen as David kept talking.

"Pop wanted the group small, so we wouldn't draw attention. He was nervous the minute we stepped on this cursed mountain, told me there was danger, said we ought to leave. And what do I do? I announce our presence by banging on danger's door and demanding entrance."

We trotted now to catch the group that was still putting space between us and whatever hunted us from the other side of the mountain. Our pace was so rapid I had to take deep breaths before asking the question that surely must have been tattooed on my forehead.

"Did you see the light?"

"We saw it night before last. It looked like the moon had fallen into the trees, but we didn't see the source until the next day. The light was dimmed by the sun, but the tower was squat, made of giant hewn rocks and fitted together like . . ." I knew he expected me to finish his sentence.

"I know," I said. "Sacsayhuaman. How close did you get?"

David shook his head and stared at his feet passing under him. "Close enough for Ram to get excited and run ahead. Close enough to bring death." He stopped still. "I was irresponsible, unprofessional, putting everyone in danger like this."

Doc turned around and yelled orders to move faster. David had requested that he take over, wanting to be relieved of leadership. But David was soon called up front to confer about direction. I looked behind us at the mountain and wondered how close you have to be to use a poisoned blow dart.

We got lost a couple of times. John shot so many snakes I got bored counting. Somebody found mashed protein bars in their pack that tasted very, very good. Our hammocks had been left behind, which was all right because we didn't dare stop for the night anyway. The stars gave enough light for traveling the plain, and the mosquito suits frustrated innumerable flying death squads. The suits rustled like taffeta dresses at a Junior Prom, which may have frightened off larger animals.

Where the grasslands and jungle met we saw faint lights in a massive tree. When we investigated, the lights turned out to be in the bodies of large spiders celebrating a kind of mating ritual. A writhing movement along the trunk extinguished the lights and a hungry snake ruined the party. We rested briefly, heads nodding, as the first shreds of daylight filtered to the jungle floor, then staggered on.

Strange memories cluttered my thinking. I relived the children's game called "Lion Hunt." "Let's go on a Lion Hunt," we'd chant, clapping our hands in rhythmic glee. "Creep through the jungle, caawwww, caawwww, caawwww!" We'd make exotic bird noises. "Across the savannah, swish, swish, swish." Our arms moved tall grass aside. "Up the mountain, puff, puff, puff," we'd pant. "Oh, look, there's a tree. Let's climb it!" Our arms reached for invisible branches in the air as we grunted and pawed our way to the top. Then someone would cry "Oh, NO! I see a lion. Run!" Screeching in delighted fear, we repeated all the actions backwards. Fall from the tree, slip down the mountain, swish across the savannah, creep through the jungle, find the vans . . . find the vans . . . find the vans . . .

The keys to one of the cars had been left in Ramiro's pack. We collapsed into the other two vans, locked the doors, and took weary turns driving. No one thought the savages would follow us once we got to the dirt track, but something compelled us to continue in spite of exhaustion.

"I can't drive anymore," John complained after the first hour. "I'm asleep at the wheel."

There was no response. Then my voice from the back

said, "I'll get us all killed if I take over."

Doc, ever willing to cooperate, offered, "Maybe I can drive for thirty minutes or so."

"No good," John said. "Let's sleep for an hour until somebody gets some energy."

"If we stop for an hour," Doc said, "both cars have to stop. Maybe someone in the other car can drive."

"It's lucky we had to leave the third van behind," I mumbled. "We couldn't have driven it between the six of us."

Nobody laughed.

CHAPTER 13

I stood in the office of the Archaeology Department. Nothing had changed. On the west wall hung a picture of the famous cracked stone face of Angkor Wat, accompanied by a sepia-toned Howard Carter at the entrance of Tut's Tomb; the department secretary's desk still had a vase full of marbles which held plastic flowers, each posy taped to a pen so there was always a supply of writing implements. The secretary herself smiled sweetly at me.

"So, you're back."

I was tempted to say "No, I'm a figment of your imagination," but secretaries are more powerful than deans. She had the ability to smooth my path or strew boulders along it. I preferred smooth, so I said amiably, "Yes, I returned four days ago."

This particular woman had a high voice and an annoying habit of beginning sentences with "so . . ."

"So . . . I hear you went to Brazil."

"That's right."

"So, what did you find?"

"Not much."

"So, somebody must have found something, or

you wouldn't have gone. Was it an old Portuguese settlement?"

"It was a false alarm."

"That figures. Brazil's a big, empty country full of jungles and aborigines. Rio de Janeiro is the only place worth seeing. So, how long were you in Brazil?"

"Only about ten days." I mentally reviewed it: a day in Brasilia, two days through the jungle to the lost city, three days there, one and a half days back to Brasilia, one day in comatose collapse, one day arranging flights . . . yup, ten days.

"Did you get to see Rio de Janeiro?"

"Uh . . . no."

"So, next time you get down there, stay in Rio and make the trip worthwhile. We were there seven years ago on vacation. You know what they say: 'See Rio once before you die!' When we went . . .'"

Her voice settled onto a mote of dust floating in the air. I could see it balanced on that speck, still hearing it like the miniscule sound of a small insect buzzing around my ear. Ramiro never saw Rio de Janeiro before he died. Pop probably didn't, either. I don't know what David told Ram's family, but the rest of the crew agreed not to speak of the city or the circumstances, since the entire venture was furtive and borderline illegal. David would have to give somebody an explanation for abandoning expensive equipment, but the city, its Sumerian connection, and the light in the jungle would join Ram, Pop, and Percy Fawcett in death. There wasn't much to say even if we could say it. A fabulous lost city was found and lost again.

I wondered if anyone would ever see the uncovered treasures I'd left on the tables, or if someone in the future would climb the black obelisk in the center of the plaza to stare into the face of the stone man. I tried to remember if I'd put the artifacts catalogue in a safe place, away from wind and rain. I hoped my tent wouldn't become a hotel for snakes and spiders, but I knew it would. It didn't matter. The flight of the bats every night would eventually shred it out of existence. Meanwhile, the light in the jungle still shone.

"... again, but it was expensive. It's a one-time vacation that everybody should have. Too bad you couldn't stay an extra week."

The department secretary looked at me for a response. I took a stab at it.

"I'll start saving now." The comment sounded weak but seemed to satisfy her. I smiled and continued, "Tell Dr. Edson I'm back early and can teach a class this semester if he wants to schedule it."

"I'll do that, Dr. Howard."

I'd gone to my university in person to touch base with reality, see the campus, walk its paths, note the humanity. Everyone was alive and well, oblivious to the events in Brazil. Four days ago I'd staggered home and dropped my zippered pack in the entry closet. The thought formed that a small, poisonous green snake could have made its way into my possessions and might unleash a Pandora's box of fear and destruction on my unsuspecting neighborhood. I shook my head. Not possible. I'd opened the pack during the trip home. Besides, there weren't any small green snakes in Brazil. They were all big. But I intended to leave the pack hidden from sight until I could face its memories.

Robert Edson called, glad to add me to the next semester's offerings. He said a freshman overview class on Middle Eastern ethnoarchaeology would be nice; could I teach two? When I hung up the phone I noticed a small blue book on the desk. That lousy little Book of Mormon was still here, and why was it on my desk when it belonged on top of the Bhagavad Gita in my library? It seemed the book could sprout legs and wander at will.

"Okay," I said aloud to the obnoxious little book, "I'll read you during the semester." The book was such a tiny little thing, I almost felt sorry for it. How could such a pathetic volume cause so much controversy? Why would anybody care?

Winter semester found me in an early morning class facing sleepy-eyed, hormonally unbalanced youngsters who had eternity ahead of them and didn't yet sense mortality breathing down their necks. "Some writing forms," I told them, "can be connected to the ancient Middle East." I explained that proper Egyptian writing begins with a *colophon,* a literary device that requires the beginning of a text to give the date, the education of the author, praise for his parentage, and the purpose for writing. "If we find an ancient parchment with a colophon," I said, "we can track it to Egyptian-Semitic origins." They dutifully took notes. Some of them yawned.

That night I picked up the little blue nemesis which had followed me like an explosive with a homing device. It was time to face it.

I Nephi, having been born of goodly parents, therefore I was taught somewhat in all the learning of my father; and having seen many afflictions in the course of my days, nevertheless, having been highly favored of the Lord in all my days; yea, having had a great knowledge of the goodness and the mysteries of God, therefore I make a record of my proceedings in my days. Yea, I make a record in the language of my father, which consists of the learning of the Jews and the language of the

Egyptians. And I know that the record which I make is true; And I make it with mine own hand; and I make it according to my knowledge. For it came to pass in the commencement of the first year of the reign of Zedekiah, king of Judah . . .

It was a genuine, unmistakable colophon. All the proper parts were there. How could a farm boy know that a formal colophon should be at the beginning of a book supposedly written by an ancient, educated man of the Middle East? He couldn't. When Nephi wrote "I make it with mine own hand," it corresponded to the Egyptian "written with mine own fingers."

As I continued reading I was impressed with the "and it came to pass" prefaces. They belonged there. Take one out and the flow of the ancient words would be strangled. The phrase is ancient Egyptian. As far back as the thirteenth century BCE, in a manuscript from the dynasty of Seti II, nearly every sentence begins with "behold" or "it came to pass." The formula is preserved today in Arabic where "I saw a dog" is bad written form. You have to write, "Behold, I saw a dog."

I looked for more Egyptian influence and found it in the names of Nephi and Sam. Laman and Lemuel, the older brothers, had Arabic origins, while Jacob and Joseph stemmed straight from Hebrew. I could guess Lehi's history by the names he gave his sons. He probably started in the desert with a caravan trade business, rose to wealth associated with Egypt, and returned to his Hebrew roots in the wilderness where his sons Jacob and Joseph were born. Philology is fun.

By the time I'd reached 2 Nephi, I knew the book wasn't composed by an American boy in the 1800s. Any fool could see that the grammar, idioms, and use of function words were Semitic. I skimmed through the phrasing, then dropped into sleep during the Isaiah sections, an indication the book might be legitimate. Any normal kid composing his own story would have found a way to bypass Isaiah and get on with the plot.

I woke a few hours later and found that the blue book had left a dent in my chin, but not in my heart. So far, the Book of Mormon represented a nice little mystery of how an uneducated twenty-four-year-old got so many things right. Who else could have written it? During the next weeks I noted additional evidence of ancient origin. Egyptian names were randomly scattered throughout the text: Zeniff, Ammon, Helaman, Korihor, Pahoran, Paanchi. The terms "did eat" and "did go" were awkward in English but correct grammar in Semitic languages. "Stiffneckedness" was literal Arabic, which the Smith boy couldn't have known. The numbering system with endless "ands" such as "forty and six, forty and seven" was unnatural in English, but nicely Semitic.

I tore through the pages, occasionally stopping to research historical curiosities: the appearance of chiasmus, another ancient literary device; Abinadi reading the ten commandments, probably embroidered on the king's clothing as patterned in the Old Testament; the custom of execution by hanging on a tree, then cutting the tree down amid ritual group recitations. Then there was the event that brought families to their temple after an earthquake leveled everything. There was even some research that indicated they may have celebrated the Feast of Tabernacles, a festival thought to be strictly Jewish. I was like a kid with a new coloring book, quickly scratching crayon pigment outside the lines, then turning the page and grabbing a new color. I wasn't terribly interested in the story line, and I didn't try to puzzle out who actually wrote the thing. But at the edge of my mind a concern formed about origins. Angels aren't academically acceptable.

My university classes ran automatically. Toward the end of the semester I gave my standard migration lecture. "Only the written word travels through time and space," I began. "If nobody wrote it, it never happened." I loved saying that sentence. It was profound. "Ancient Near Eastern epics tell of massive migrations that were set in motion 4,000 years ago, caused in part by weather patterns and warfare. Fortunately for us, scribes wrote about it and left clay tablets for us to find, and now we know that ancient people swarmed to find new places to settle, bringing dramatic changes all over the known world."

That night I began the Book of Ether. The Jaredites migrated in classic fashion, most likely across Asia judging from descriptions of the time required and the large lakes they crossed. I accessed my memory files to dredge up a conversation with James, the young Mormon archaeologist, about Caucasian graves strung across China dating to 2000 BCE. I'd read the reports and vaguely remembered mention of a six-foot tall male mummy sporting a blond beard; another had red braids. They buried their horses, which had marks on the teeth from bit wearing, indicating the horses were broken and trained.

The story continued with the Jaredites reaching the ocean and constructing eight enclosed barges. The brother of Jared, whose name was footnoted as Moriancumer, asked God for light, and God said, "What would ye that I should prepare for you?" This was an unusual God who left important decisions to mere mortals. Thus encouraged, Moriancumer carved out sixteen stones, expecting that if God touched them, they would shine. What prompted him to think of stones? Why trouble himself to carve them out when he could just pick up rocks from the ground? Did they have to be transparent like, say, crystal? Some interesting details were missing from the story, but on Mount Shelem God honored the man's request and gave him light from stones.

Aha! Light from stones!

I'd come full circle back to the legend of China's T'ai Shan, where a great leader came down carrying shining rocks. Even the names Shelem and Shan were a short 4,000-year linguistic leap. I put the book in my lap to look up at the ceiling, thoughts churning through possibilities. Moriancumer might have known about the drowned civilization, which produced lights from crystals. That kind of information makes itself permanent folklore. When God gave him responsibility for choosing, the man reached into his background and asked for a reproduction of the ancient technology and . . . I stopped.

Wait a minute.

Wait just a minute.

The point wasn't crystals or lights or advanced civilizations. The point was . . . the brother of Jared saw Jesus Christ. The whole Book of Mormon was about Jesus Christ.

Months ago I had collapsed on a ledge and expressed gratitude to a god I didn't know. Now I was reading about an ancient nomad who saw Jesus Christ at the beginning of recorded time. His story was in a book translated by a young man who said he also saw Christ, along with God the Father. What was I supposed to do with this?

I finished the remaining thirty-eight pages of the Book of Mormon but couldn't apply Moroni's promise in 10:4 because I hadn't actually read the book.

Okay, I'd read the book.

But I'd missed the message.

I started over and took notes. Seven weeks later I called the telephone number written in ink on the inside of the book's title page.

"Hello?" It was a woman's voice.

"Hello. Is James the archeologist there?"

She laughed. "I'll find him."

A pause. A man's voice.

"Hello?"

"James, this is the old lady from T'ai Shan."

"Dr. Howard! I'll bet you've read my book."

"I have."

"And you want to know what to do next."

"I do."

"Well, look in the yellow pages under 'Church of Jesus Christ of Latter-day Saints,' and—"

"It won't be under 'Rattle-day Snakes'?" I cut in.

He laughed.

"It won't. Find 'Arizona Mission Office' and request an appointment with two Elders."

"Elders?"

"The name is strange. They're actually young."

I decided not to let the play on words distract me "Then what do I do?"

"Do what your heart tells you."

A week later my doorbell rang. Two grinning young men with short hair, shiny shoes, and knotted ties stood on my porch.

"Dr. Howard, we presume?"

"Mormon missionaries, I presume?"

I invited them in.

CHAPTER 14

"Mom!"

"Marisa!" I switched the phone to my left hand and settled onto a kitchen counter chair, knowing the conversation would be a long one. "I'd recognize your voice anywhere!"

"Well, you should. You've been my mom since I was two."

"It's made my life worth living. To what do I owe this welcome connection?" Marisa usually called every Sunday to play catch-up, but a few weeks had gone by.

"I have the best news! I haven't called you until I was sure. It will make you jump up and click your heels. You'll waltz around the room humming a lullaby. I'm giving you a grandchild!"

A grandchild. Was I old enough to have a grandchild? Yes. Was I mentally and emotionally ready for a grandchild? Probably not. Should I tell Marisa I wasn't ready? How do you prepare for this? I swallowed surprise at my feelings and responded positively.

"Oh, Marisa, that's much better than the best news. It's a gargantuan . . ." I fished for the old words we used when Marisa was a child. ". . . a gargantuan, megalithic anomaly!" She laughed her wonderful bubble of a laugh. It warmed me to my toenails, and I asked, "When does this incredible thing happen to us?" I relinquished the phone to her so she could tell me details, doctor's orders, plans for a nursery, and whether or not they wanted to know the gender before birth. Potential names were placed on hold pending that decision.

"Maybe we should wait to see when the little one gets here," she said. "I love surprises."

"Well," I said gently, "I have a surprise of my own. Certainly not as grand as yours, but . . . I'm thinking of joining the Mormon Church."

The silence was so deafening I thought the line had gone dead. But apparently only Marisa had gone dead.

"Marisa? Are you there?"

"This is a joke, right? Please don't tell me you read that Book of Mormon the strange kid in China gave you."

"Of course not. Well, not at first. I just put it in my library. There are a lot of strange books in my library . . ."

Marisa quickly quoted my own words, "But you only collect them, you don't believe them."

I offered excuses. "A whole series of events pushed me into reading it. This book is different. I've been meeting with the Mormon missionaries and they're very persuasive." I gave a laugh that didn't have enough energy to last two seconds.

"Mom, you're a weird lady. It's part of who you are and sometimes your eccentricities are cute. But this one isn't and I won't support you."

I stood and paced. "Marisa, let me explain. There are a hundred reasons why I shouldn't join, and only one reason why I should, but . . ."

"Let me add one more reason to the hundred: your grandchild."

"My membership in a church won't—"

"No, Mom, I'm going to say this. I can't have my child influenced by a grandmother who belongs to a dangerous cult."

"Don't be silly! It's not a cult. You'd be amazed—"

"Cult, Mom. It's a cult. Even other cults can't out-cult the Mormons. I won't expose my child to it. He or she will simply never know you. So now you've got a hundred and one reasons why you shouldn't join those people."

My legs were suddenly weak, and I leaned against the wall. "Please give me a chance to tell you about it."

"I've said my piece. I love you, Mom, but I don't think I like you."

She hung up.

I slid to the floor. The phone lay on the carpet next to me, beeping its monotonous busy signal while I squandered my entire tear duct storage. Then a strange piece of mental maneuvering filtered through my pain and dredged up a replay of the departure from Brazil. The team had said somber good-byes as they separated. John and I caught our flight to Arizona and settled into silence. Two hours out of Washington, D.C., he spoke beyond cursory requirements.

"Do you remember that media nightmare over the age of the Sphinx?"

"I remember it, but I'm sure nobody else does. It was a long time ago."

"He was right."

"Excuse me?"

"My graduate student was right. The Sphinx wasn't constructed during Chephren's reign in the twenty-fifth century BCE. It's a lot older and one clue is in its weather patterns. The Sphinx has been covered with sand for most of the last

five thousand years, so it wasn't the wind blowing sand that weathered it."

I had waited for John to continue but he didn't. After a count of four I figured it was a test to see if I was really listening, like a conversation with a teenager.

"If it wasn't sand, John," I said, "then what weathered the Sphinx?"

"Water. A lot of it. There hasn't been that much water in Egypt since 8000 BCE. The Valley Temple at Giza was also weathered by water, along with the Osireion at Abydos. Egyptologists don't like it, but geologists are into the act now, and they don't care about pre-figured, inviolate timetables. Ergo . . ." John paused and turned to me. I met his gaze with all the attention I could muster, determined not to smile at his use of "ergo" to make his point. John faced forward again. "It means there was an advanced civilization that predates Egypt by thousands of years."

John might have expected me to be surprised, shocked, or even amused at this outrageous concept, but it fit nicely with the tale told by the Tibetan Monk in Thailand, and I nudged John forward with the words "Keep going." He glanced at me with narrowed eyes, not sure if I was patronizing or sincere, since he'd seldom seen me sincere. "Really," I nodded. "I'm with you on this, and I'm fascinated." He talked faster, as if he had to hurry in case I wouldn't listen long enough for him to finish.

"There's other evidence that Chephren didn't build the Sphinx. The Inventory Stele tells that Cheops built a temple next to the Sphinx, which was before Chephren's time. The facts are there for anyone who looks. But I didn't want to point my finger, make the announcement, and ruin my career. So I destroyed my graduate student instead, even though I knew he was right. Acceptance was more important to me than . . ." his lips tightened slightly, ". . . than the truth."

I waited a respectful moment, then felt the need to respond. "Truth is very subjective," I said, "especially in the world of science." Stupid response.

"I regret it." John spoke the words with no emotion, like an aging zombie. "Others are picking up the pieces I dropped, speaking out, saying what needs to be heard, standing with the evidence. I betrayed myself."

"I would have done the same thing, John," I said. "I would have done exactly the same thing."

The hypnotic sound of the busy signal brought me back to the floor of my kitchen. I scooped up the phone, hauled myself to the counter, and replaced the receiver.

"There are a hundred and one reasons why I should not join this church," I said to my gray granite counter, "and only one why I should. It's true."

The baptism ceremony was short. The young "Elders" dunked me under the water, brought me up, dried me off, and told me to be at church on Sunday. Two weeks later the Bishop asked if I'd accept a call to the nursery, a holding pen for children until they're old enough to go to Primary, the children's organization. And that's how, three weeks into being a Mormon, I found myself with a crying child on my lap, two others wobbling around the room, and miniature tow-headed male twins hitting each other with colorful plastic toys.

"I have a doctorate in ethnoarchaeology," I told the toddlers.

Oh, well.

Enough time passed that the loss of my daughter evolved to a dull ache. I talked to others who had experienced pain when they changed their lives. Misery meeting company usually results in mutual misery, but in a gospel setting the effect was benign and I was comforted.

Being single in a married church was sometimes awkward. Social events required me to sit with other women rather than be integrated with couples, but I found conversation among the women delightful, and in six months I moved from rocking babies to teaching in the Relief Society, the adult women's group. The assignment required me to search deep into my fledgling faith and I realized the maligned church I'd joined could be a lifetime study. It became clear that the genius of this church was its unpaid ministry, which offered leadership experience to every member.

In spite of my growing testimony, I said nothing about the Church to my university colleagues and hoped the subject wouldn't follow me into the ivy halls. Losing my daughter was more than should be required. I needed to protect the respect I had in my profession. I apologized to God and asked Him to understand.

I knew He was disappointed.

The phone rang on a Saturday morning while I cleaned out a closet, having been admonished to do so and, indeed, given written instructions for such cleaning during the last Relief Society Enrichment meeting. It was not in my nature to clean. I welcomed the interruption.

"This is not a recording," I answered. "Speak to me."

"Mom?"

My throat moved into my heart.

"Marisa!" The sound of her voice was so beautiful that I leaned against a wall to support my happiness.

"Mom, we have a little girl. She was born two weeks ago."

"I figured the baby had arrived. I've kept track of the months and thought of you every day." I was going to say I'd prayed for her safety but decided this was not the time. Shut up, old lady. Let the girl talk.

"We've named her Annie, after Mo's mother. I hope that doesn't hurt your feelings."

"'Matilda' and 'Matt' are not names to foist on a little girl," I laughed. "'Annie' is a better choice." This was small talk leading to large talk. Stay calm.

Marisa threw herself into a dialogue that must have been practiced but fell apart as she stumbled across her words. "Well, I decided to call because I was visiting the archaeology department and saw a dig report I knew you'd be interested in, at least I thought you'd be interested, or I hoped you'd be interested and I kept thinking about it . . . and about you . . . and decided to call. Maybe you won't be interested but, you know, you never know until you ask . . ." Her voice faltered. I picked up the slack.

"You are the cutest thing to be looking out for me. Please tell me everything, start at the beginning and finish at the end."

It turned out to be an excavation in Belize, funded by a Texas development company planning to build a tourist resort. They had purchased land containing ruins, intending to reconstruct the ancient pyramids, plazas, and ball courts as an exquisite backdrop for their hotels, restaurants, and swimming pools. I thought the idea was an abomination, but interjected appropriate "reallys" and "fascinatings," which encouraged her to continue.

She said the archeologists had found evidence of a dramatic transformation from a primitive fishing community to a cosmopolitan center, including a hydraulic system of canals and drainage ditches, all built suddenly on top of the existing village.

"I'd love to read the report," I gushed. She offered to send the narrative, along with information about future seasons.

"Please send a picture of Annie, too," I requested. There was a pause, long enough to be uncomfortable. I stopped breathing, waiting for her response.

"Mom," she said. "I've missed you. I want to talk to you again. We can't talk religion, though."

"Agreed," I said. "We have a lifetime of things in common and a plethora of subjects to discuss. Welcome home."

She was pleased. I was ecstatic. All's well that ends well.

Usually.

The Belize report came in the mail. I blessed the yellow paperbound volume, then tossed it on a pile in the garage. When Marisa called again she described Annie's wonderful smile, her skill in tracking objects, the silly way Mo tilted his head when he looked at his daughter, and after we'd exhausted the important topics she said, "So . . . are you going?"

"Going where?"

"To Belize. Did you read the report?"

"Well, of course, and enjoyed every minute." My conscience kicked my ribs. I used to take pride in my considerable ability to tell a decent lie, but I couldn't pull it off anymore. Being a Mormon was inconvenient.

"Did you get the names and numbers and everything you need?" She was going to push it. Oh me, oh my.

"Yes, I did. Everything is on my desk as we speak." Another whopper. *Archaeology at Cerros* gathered cobwebs in my garage as we spoke. But my relationship with Marisa was at stake, and honesty was not the best policy.

I blundered on. "I planned to call sometime this week and see if I could join the team." Liar, liar, pants on fire.

"I'm really glad, Mom. When I saw the reports, I knew you'd want to hear about it."

Uh-huh.

I retrieved the volume from the grimy garage, hoping the Relief Society wouldn't give a handout on garage cleaning, rattled the papers to scare out spiders, and returned to my desk. After quickly skimming the report I called the number to immediately cleanse myself of my lies. A woman answered by announcing her name as Dr. Gart. I played the introduction game, gave my credentials, and followed by saying, "I've read the interim report on Cerros and would like to join the team for . . .uh . . .a few weeks." A few weeks seemed reasonable, long enough and short enough. I could handle it.

"Dr. Howard, I am genuinely sorry to tell you that our funds have dried to a bare trickle. We're scrambling to raise money to complete current excavations."

"What happened to the Texas corporation that hired you for the initial survey?"

"They ran into so much red tape that they finally gave up and deeded the property back to the Belizean government. I suppose they'll write it off as a bad business investment."

It was my cue to exit gracefully. I could tell Marisa how disappointed I was, how sad that the opportunity was snatched from me. The whole thing had panned out perfectly.

Instead, I heard a voice, sounding suspiciously like my own, saying, "Tell you what. I'll pay my own way. I'd like to see the place and contribute what I can."

Zounds! I'd gone insane.

CHAPTER 15

At the Belize City airport, a short brown man with a yellow grin agreed to take me to the village of Chunox, two hours away. His wretched rusted taxi looked as good as any in the line, and I had no fear of the Belizean native who cricked his neck to look up at me. He knew instinctively what I was capable of. We communicated in the international language of dollar signs and bargained for a price. His English proved about the level of my Spanish so conversation was sparse, which was a good thing. The jaw-jarring drive over deeply pitted dirt roads would have broken our teeth if we'd been talking.

Chunox was a combination Mayan village and Hispanic community, grass huts mingled with cinderblock structures. Children at the Seventh Day Adventist School wore dark blue uniforms as they squealed at games played in the dirt. My instructions were to find a man named Antonio who supervised native workers from surrounding villages. He was expecting me. We climbed into his little wooden boat for the hour journey to Lowry's Bight, a narrow spit of swampy land extending into Chetumal Bay. Antonio's outboard motor set up a clatter that reached pandemonium proportions, so we traveled the brown river in silence until we finally entered the bay. Skirting the peninsula, I caught the vision of a rough rock pyramid peeking above the trees to our left.

We followed the northern shoreline to a dilapidated dock where a woman stood waiting. She must have heard Antonio's motor ten minutes earlier across the water.

"Welcome to Cerros, Dr. Howard. I'm Dr. Gart." She looked to be in her early forties, brown hair chopped in a short, no-nonsense style. The loose, lightweight beige pants and shirt showed sweat stains in all the places people sweat. She was smiling. I figured she had reason to smile: she was getting my expertise free of charge. Furthermore, I'd agreed to spend a few evenings as a guest lecturer. I still wasn't sure how I'd gotten into this mess, but it would only be two weeks. The reward for my labor was a stop in Chicago to visit Marisa and meet my newborn granddaughter. I'd gone to Cerros first as a conversation starter . . . in case we needed one.

Dr. Gart gave me her welcome speech. "It's an honor to have you here," she said. "I studied your book in undergraduate school and thought it was so good I didn't resell it."

My estimation of the woman rose a notch. "I apologize for the sleepless nights it must have caused you," I said. "I hope I can make it up by being of some use here."

Formalities finished, she led me off the dock, leaving Antonio to unload and haul my equipment. An unaccustomed feeling of guilt prompted me to take my wheeled bag. Antonio raised his eyebrows in surprise.

"No, no, Señora Doctor, I am able."

"I know you're able, Antonio, but if I help, we can do this in one trip and save you from coming back."

"I am easy to come back," he said.

"But I hope you'll show me the work you're doing when we get to the site," I said. "And I don't want to waste time." The changes in me were scary. In the old days I wouldn't have noticed native help unless they were worth interviewing, but it took no effort to be nice these days. Who would'a thought?

Antonio nodded, expressed gratitude, and said, "I am happy to show to you my dig."

I'd made a friend. As it turned out, my insignificant gesture would pay hefty dividends later.

Dr. Gart guided us down a wide trail cut through tight, tangled trees. "We made the path eight feet wide to accommodate a small backhoe we were able to buy when cash flow was better," she explained. "We've carved trenches across the site to establish the old village location."

A buzzing sound drew my attention to a hoard of mosquitoes surrounding me like a black shroud, guests at an anticipated blood banquet. My repellent formed an invisible barrier, but they were ready. Gart noticed my study of the tiny creatures. "This place is a serious swamp," she warned. "Don't let your repellent wear off. The mosquitoes rival any in Maya country."

Two weeks, I thought. *It's only two weeks. I can do this.*

Gart pointed to areas behind dense trees. "Over there we've discovered parts of the canal used to drain the swamp, obviously not built by the original villagers. Skilled architects must have designed it, along with the pyramids."

My eye caught the movement of a hand-sized hairy spider, its bright vermillion body scampering into a dense growth of vines. "Was that an electric orange tarantula?" I said.

"Yes. They don't bite very often. Anyway, they're easy to see. Other bugs are not so noticeable. We have good first-aid for scorpions and army ants."

Two weeks. Two weeks. Two weeks. Can I do this?

"Not all dangerous things move," she said as she pointed to a black tree rising above its neighbors. "This is poisonwood. The natives call it Chachem. If you brush against the bark or the leaves, or if it drips dew on you, it'll burn whatever it touches . . . turns your skin black, you swell up—so don't go leaning against it."

Two weeks, I groaned to myself. *I can't do this.*

Gart kept up the tour guide chatter. "We opened up extensive exposures which date exclusively to the Late Preclassic period. We hope you can confirm pottery chronology."

I stopped walking and looked at her. "Late Preclassic is 300 BCE. That would make Cerros older than Chichen Itza, Palenque, and El Mirador."

"That's right," she said. "We think we've got something special here."

The path took us around a mound of shrubs and trees and then abruptly opened into a massive clearing. Three pyramids of differing design and size spread themselves before us. Human workers crawled on them, clearing the pyramids like ants pushing debris. Two additional mounds still dressed in dirt and foliage beckoned through southern trees not yet leveled. A ball court could be discerned in the distance. I stood on the spot, awed by the scene rising from the dust. Turning to Gart, I felt the formation of a foolish grin on my face.

"How big is the site?" I asked.

"We estimate about fifty-three acres. I see you've noticed the ball court. There are two of them. Cerros is one of the few Preclassic sites with ball courts."

"The interim report was too modest."

"We didn't need to generate interest since the project was private."

Two weeks! I thought. *Only two weeks to discover what this place is.*

"Well, Dr. Gart," I said. "I'm glad I came."

A dozen native workers busily uncovered a five-story structure behind us. Four decorative masks, as tall as the men standing next to them, could be partially seen on the sides of the central steps. Two staging areas, one above the other, flanked the stairs halfway up, and I imagined the spectacles that once held power over the audience on the plaza below. Shakespeare at his finest couldn't have outdone these guys.

"This is Structure Six," Gart said. "Pyramid Four is a little larger, but this one is a masterpiece, extraordinarily decorated with symbols of power that seem connected to Olmec art. This season we're doing a vertical excavation to analyze construction fill. The platform on top can accommodate an eight-foot exposure. It's Antonio's project." She motioned for Antonio to bring my supplies and then said to me, "You'll want to set up camp. I'll arrange a meeting with the rest of the team later this evening."

Antonio and I chose a spot and, as we struggled with my newly purchased tent, I mourned my domicile left behind in Brazil. We finally pulled out the paperwork and snapped the parts together. When all else fails, read the directions.

Antonio led me to his pyramid and gallantly helped me traverse the steep, skinny steps. Halfway up I leaned over to catch a breath and caught sight of a large, straw-colored scorpion, a mass of squirming babies clinging to her back as she lumbered across the stones. I made a mental note not to sit on the pyramids for any length of time. Then I amended it to remind me not to sit anywhere for any length of time.

At the top I walked to the edge of an eight-foot square excavation that reached down seven feet. Two ladders leaned against opposite walls.

"Please be careful, Señora Doctor," Antonio warned. "Already two men fall. We need wood sticks to make nobody fall."

"A fence," I offered.

"*Jes,* what you say."

"And what do you look for while the men dig this hole?"

"If we see the jade carved, the hammer of stone, or what Dr. Gart say a 'layer,' then I call to her."

"And have you found anything like that?"

"On top was found jade in pieces, things people use for to cook and to hunt, even gold. But now only dirt, big rocks, little rocks."

I smiled. "I'd like to see the dirt, big rocks, and little rocks."

We descended. The ladder moved like a bungee cord. Native workers constructed it on the site, with extensions as needed. When it stopped quivering, I checked the walls around me. There was no layering to indicate gradual development. Curioser and curioser.

That evening the team, which amounted to seven people, assembled to meet me and talk about the dig.

A young man with acne started. "At first we expected Classic remains, like at Tikal and Palenque, but there weren't any." I glanced at the group. There wasn't a wrinkle among them. Why was everyone so young? "After some wildcat sampling," he continued, "we found an offering at the top of Structure Six. Everything dated to Late Preclassic."

A girl with hair in braids, held behind her neck by a leather thong, said, "When we uncovered the masks on the stairs they looked similar to one in Uaxactun. The question is, which is older?"

Dr. Gart interjected. "We hope Dr. Howard can supply that answer."

A skinny kid with a dozen five-inch straggly black hairs hanging off his chin spoke. "The polychrome paint, the use of outset stairways, the huge masks," he waved his arms to take in the site, "the whole sophistication of the place, not to mention the chronology, shows that Cerros is the beginning of Mayan civilization." It was spoken with the self-assurance of the very young.

"We can't conclude that until further testing," Dr. Gart chided. Then she shook her head and rubbed the back of her neck, a sure sign of a disclaimer. "But it's a fact that over two thousand years ago Cerros served as a major ceremonial center built squarely on top of an existing village."

I agreed with her. "I saw the excavation on Structure Six this afternoon," I said. "It's all loose boulder fill, clean marl capping, and only one construction episode so far. The place went up fast."

"Quarries for construction have been found a few meters southeast of here." It was another youngster, a girl in shorts and halter top. She really needed clothing to protect her skin from sun and bugs. A few more trial seasons and she'd figure it out.

Suddenly, the answer hit. These archeologists were

graduate students, working for credit, experience, or thesis projects. Lack of funding eliminated experienced professionals, leaving Dr. Gart as the exclusive head of a group of natives and a gaggle of adolescents.

Gart leaned toward the group, arms across her knees. "Something big happened here," she said. "It violates the rules of diffusion and, even more surprising, gradual evolution and spread and consolidation, which is standard thought in modern archaeology. We have a nice little mystery on our hands."

Everybody grinned.

Something that breaks rules, I thought, *has all my attention.*

When the meeting was finished, Dr. Gart walked me to my tent.

"Dr. Howard, I just want to make sure you understand my position." She spread her palms in front of her to emphasize that she was going to tell me her position. "I've been placed in charge and the responsibility is mine. Even though you have the credentials, I'd appreciate it if you'd avoid any public dialogues with me that might undermine my authority."

"I understand your position," I said, "and I don't intend to take over your project." I nearly told her the whole thing was just an excuse to get to Chicago and repair a rift with my daughter, but it wasn't true anymore. The place pulled at my soul like a spirit magnet under my skin. Instead I added, "I'm only here for two weeks." The chat with Gart bothered me. I realized she was not only the project director, she was a professor with no one to dispute her opinion. She had absolute power, the kind that destroys absolutely.

For ten days I studied rituals of termination. People had broken their belongings . . . jade jewelry, obsidian tools, clay and ceramic pots . . . and buried their house sites in a ceremony to rid themselves of an old life and start a new one. Based on samples from village trenches and pyramid summits, the inhabitants of the village had united in a massive construction effort which ended just two generations later. It was behavioral archaeology in action, from father to grandson. The anthropologist in me was intrigued. Someone or something had been introduced that caused people to inexplicably change from a primitive lifestyle to a complicated social and spatial organization. The transition required construction of five massive pyramids with plazas and ball courts.

I sat on my haunches and sifted through the soil for clues. The reward was dirt under my fingernails. At night, mosquitoes sung their vicious lullaby, and I fell into dreams like the two workers down Antonio's hole.

CHAPTER 16

Day eleven. Noon.

I sat at a long table and pieced together parts of a jade talisman. A hole bored through the head showed the item had been a necklace, but the left ear was missing. As I pawed through rubble in a box, a male voice spoke behind me.

"Señora Doctor?"

"Hello, Antonio. Have you found something?" It was our standard greeting. We both knew his excavation didn't yield anything and his answer was always, "Just dirt, big rocks, little rocks." But this time was different.

"Yes, Señora. You will please to come?"

His face lacked its characteristic smile. Something worried him. I pushed myself up from the table and stepped across the bench.

"Lead the way," I said.

We walked to Structure Six where the plaza held a dozen men, standing idly in small groups, a buzz of talk darting among them. I thought I caught the Spanish word "luz," light, but my Spanish wasn't reliable. I brushed it off.

We climbed to the vertical excavation sunk through

the top of the pyramid. The same two homemade ladders still disappeared into the pit, but they were longer now. Antonio swung his leg across one, nodding his head toward the other for me, and began his descent. I peered into the twenty-foot abyss and then followed Antonio's example.

Every ten wobbly steps, while waiting for the ladder to settle, I studied the labor Antonio's men had done, digging by hand, hauling baskets of dirt to the top, breathing in dust and choking it out. The sun overhead made it possible to see, but when I reached bottom I was glad Antonio's flashlight showed the final ladder rung. He was on his knees, peering at something in the southeast wall.

"Here," he said. "How do you think?" He moved away to make room, focused his flashlight at a spot on the wall, and then turned it off. I kneeled where he indicated and felt sharp rocks dig through my skin. A two-inch crack in the wall caught my attention and I peeked in, drew back, placed my hands like a funnel around my face, and examined the spot again.

"Antonio," I said. "I see a light."

"*Jes.*"

"Well, it can't be a light."

"*Jes.*"

"Did you check the outside wall to see if a hole lets sunshine inside?"

"*Jes.*"

I waited. He stared at me solemnly. I lost patience.

"Antonio! Was there an opening in the outside wall?"

"No."

I looked through the large crack again, went into scholarly shock, and couldn't think clearly enough to ask a comprehensible question. "Where are we?" I said stupidly.

I meant in relation to the outside building.

Antonio answered in the only way he could. "We are here." he spoke in a worried tone, but the worry wasn't because of my question.

He was frightened.

I lowered my head and grimaced, glad Antonio couldn't see my agitation. When I stood, I had a casual smile for him, designed to reassure.

"This is interesting," I said, as if it were within possibility to find a light inside a 2,000-year-old pyramid. "Where is this spot on the outside of the structure?"

Antonio relaxed. "It is under the big faces."

Precise measurements would have to be made, but I guessed the light, or whatever it was, must be below the lowest platform, a fourth of the way up the pyramid.

"Have you told Dr. Gart?"

"No. First I tell to you to see and say like me, 'It is a light.' When I show Dr. Gart, sometime things go away . . . gold, jade, go." I wished I hadn't heard that. Antonio continued. "Also, my brother Ephron, he dig here and find the light. But he have past stories, he look for treasure, he tell the men his stories. Dr. Gart no believe. Ephron is fear Dr. Gart say he trick this place."

"You mean," I said to be sure, "Dr. Gart might think Ephron put a light down this hole?"

Antonio shrugged. "He say stories too much. But this time, he say not."

I blessed that first day when I had pulled my own wheeled suitcase along the path and later showed an interest in Antonio's work. The friendship that developed had prompted him to show me his discovery. Otherwise, Gart might have discounted the light as a joke, filled the crack with debris to prevent rumors, and I never would have known.

"I don't have authority to make decisions," I said. "You need to get Dr. Gart down here."

Antonio nodded and monkeyed his way up the ladder. I figured I shouldn't be in the hole when Gart arrived, so I climbed out, inspected the top step of the pyramid for things that bite, and sat down to scan the scene. The men below were still squatting on the ground, waiting for someone to explain the unexplainable. In the southern distance, ruins of a ball court showed the edge of stone hoops embedded in the walls. Gallery seats had been built above the court for crowds to view the game, where winners were cheered and losers beheaded. Or it might have been the other way around. Motivation like that guaranteed a good game.

West of the ball court, treetops billowed out, like green clouds beneath me, bumping their way across the landscape. My peripheral vision caught movement in the clearing below and I looked down to see Antonio and Gart walking to the stone steps. She ordered the men back to work in clearing the plaza, then tackled the pyramid. She was in good shape, taking the steep stairway like a teenager, keeping pace with Antonio as they talked animatedly. She was young, spry, knew more Spanish than I did, and had her own project site. I felt like a slug. When they reached the top step, she stopped and looked down on me for the splittest of seconds.

"What are you doing here?" she said.

"Enjoying the view," I replied sweetly.

She knew I'd seen the light first. It irked her. She swept past me, mounted one ladder as Antonio positioned himself on the other, and the two of them disappeared into the void.

Deep breaths of jungle air calmed my spinning

thoughts. There was a lousy light inside the pyramid. Macaws screamed to each other through the trees, as if announcing the aberrant behavior of the anomalous light. From my elevated perch I could spy on all the groups shoveling, sweeping, sorting, and sifting. I waited for Gart to emerge from the depths with either an answer or an excuse. It took no time. She must have glanced in the lighted crack and started back quickly. The two of them moved onto the pyramid plateau at the same time.

"It's not a light," Gart said to Antonio, but the fact she used English meant she was speaking to me as well. "Ephron is playing a joke on you. Go down and tell him it won't work." Antonio descended the steps ahead of us.

I stood to face her.

"It looks like a light to me."

"Well, it isn't." She started down. I followed behind, figuring if I tripped, she could break my fall.

"Those men down there saw a light," I said.

"No, they didn't."

"It still has to be explained." I tried to sound friendly.

"I've just explained it," she shot back. "Ephron got tired of digging and dropped a small flashlight down there."

"That's a good guess," I said, "assuming Ephron had the money to buy an expensive LED and was willing to throw it down a hole for laughs."

Gart bowed her head, like she was praying for strength, which I somehow doubted. She turned to me. The woman was stressed.

"Maybe you can hazard some alternatives before I face everybody."

"The truth is always a good choice," I said. "I know I saw a light and I'll admit it. You know you saw a light; will you deny it?"

"It isn't a light!" She began jumping two steps down at a time and I concentrated on keeping up with her until we reached the lower stage area. The four huge, elaborate masks had presided over mesmerizing theater in the past. Now, they provided a dramatic backdrop for our discussion.

"Let's consider possibilities," I offered. "There might be a hole in the side wall and we're seeing sunshine through the crack. How about a contest? The first one to find an outside opening gets the day off . . . with pay."

She grunted, which showed she didn't approve but she was listening.

"How about," she said, "suggesting there's a small room with some water that's leaked inside and the sun's shining on it?" It was a desperate idea.

"We still need sun through a hole on the outside," I reminded her.

"Look," she said, her eyes flashed anger. "You know as well as I do that if there's a light in there, the site has been contaminated. My work is destroyed. Nothing here will be taken seriously, and this place is too important for that to happen."

She was right, of course. Gart couldn't possibly explain illumination inside an ancient pyramid. The scientific community would never accept it. Her only chances at publication would be *The National Enquirer* or *Isaac Asimov's Science Fiction Magazine*. The lady was in a pickle. I thought of poor John, who didn't have courage to say the Sphinx was older than anybody believed. He couldn't risk ridicule and sarcasm from his peers.

"Maybe," I said, feeling perverse and taking a chance, "It's a sacred stone that gives illumination, handed down from an ancient civilization."

"You mean like phosphorescence?"

"Not exactly."

"Give me a break. Phosphorescence still requires an outside light source. My idea about a reflection from water makes better sense."

"Let's meet here tonight and take another look. If there's still something shining, then at least we can eliminate sunlight as a cause."

"You really aren't obligated to involve yourself in this," she said.

"It's too late, Dr. Gart. I'm involved. In fact, you have no idea how heavily invested I am with strange lights in exotic places."

She looked at me quizzically, but I didn't choose to fill in those blanks. "You go on ahead," I finished. "I need to slow down." I didn't want to imply approval by standing next to her when she made announcements.

I watched her descend and gather the crew. She spoke to Antonio, he relayed a message, and the crowd of men had dispersed by the time I stood on the plaza next to her.

"What did you tell them?" I asked.

"I told them to quit early and come back tomorrow. We'll decide the next step tonight." I didn't know if "we" was a generic term or if she included me in her statement. I assumed the latter.

"Good. What time shall we meet?"

"You really don't have to bother . . ." she began.

"I really do," I said softly.

"Well, then . . . ten o'clock will be a good time. Everyone will be asleep."

I agreed and walked to my tent, but I didn't trust Gart. I needed to protect whatever was in that pyramid. The story of the third little pig and the big bad wolf skittered through my memory; the wolf says to meet at eight and the little pig gets up earlier, picks the apples, and locks his door before the wolf gets there. Fairy tales may be for children, but they come in handy for adults. Therefore, nine o'clock found me and my flashlight stumbling across the clearing to Structure Six, searching for hairy spiders or pregnant scorpions along the way.

The hike up the pyramid is best left untold, but I rested a bit before grasping a ladder to test its wobble. Tucking my flashlight under my chin, I stepped into the darkness to locate the first rung when a light crested the top of the pyramid. I froze.

A woman's voice called out, "Who's there?"

"It is I, the third little pig," I sang out. She actually laughed. Apparently, both of us were familiar with the third pig's trick of coming earlier than agreed. I wondered which of us would be the big bad wolf.

The humor of our situation developed a kind of friendly antagonism between us as we concentrated on finding each rung of our ladders. We met at the bottom of Antonio's excavation, flashlights beaming around the walls.

"The acid test," I said.

"On three we turn off the switch," she suggested.

"And," I added, "we hope everything is pitch black."

She counted.

We turned the flashlights off.

A gentle golden light oozed itself through the southeast wall to illuminate the opposite side, slightly higher than the light source, in keeping with its tilt. Gart sunk in on herself, shoulders bowed as she backed into the wall perpendicular to the light. The tiny piece of radiance skimmed across her knees and she stared at it.

"I'm firing Ephron tomorrow," she said.

"If it's a small flashlight, the batteries will wear down. You could wait it out."

"I can't wait. Word will get around and cause wild speculation. Besides, I didn't mention a light today and my students will wonder why."

"Word will get out anyway. The men already know."

Gart's head drooped. "What am I going to do?" It looked like she was addressing her feet. I hoped her feet would give her an answer, because I didn't have one. When she raised her eyes to look at me, I knew she needed advice.

"Maybe you should shut down the project and ask some colleagues to come and take a look."

"I can't do that," she said. "I'd look like an amateur sniveling for help. Besides, we don't have the money to pay consultants. Anyway, it isn't a light." She said the words as she stared at the light.

"You're not an amateur," I said. "Neither am I. I'll stand with you."

"You aren't listening. I don't want to ask for help. As for you, if you weren't here I could throw dirt down that crack and be done with it."

I ignored the comment, since there wasn't much I could say, and instead focused on her fears.

"If you ask for other opinions, besides mine, what will happen?"

"We'll have to tear out the southeast wall to find out what it is. If it's a flashlight, I'll be humiliated."

"For the sake of argument, what will happen if it isn't a flashlight?"

"You mean like your science fiction rock?"

"No, I mean like an unexplainable light."

"Dr. Howard," she said. "Just for a minute, be reasonable. Electricity wasn't invented two thousand years ago."

"Humor me. What will happen?"

She blew out a disgusted breath and said, "Whatever it is, it'll be put in a shoebox and buried in a museum basement. Everybody will eventually forget about it. Meantime, because the site will take on prominence, someone else will be assigned to the Cerros project. I lose either way."

She was right. I felt sorry for her.

"Look," I said, "this is your dig, your find, your career. Sleep on it. The answer will come to you."

In my previous life I would have held the heavy hand of age and experience on her neck and tried to bully her into my preference. Now, I only said, "Whatever you decide, I'm behind you." It was the right thing to say.

We made our way up the ladders, down the pyramid, across the plaza, and into our tents without mishap. I couldn't sleep, and instead read my Book of Mormon.

I knew what the light was.

CHAPTER 17

Day twelve.
I stayed away from Structure Six and concentrated on my own assignments. The student team had apparently not been informed about the light since they showed no particular interest in peering into Antonio's excavation. Native workers, however, busily scooped out the southeast wall of the pyramid, carefully dislodging caprock coral blocks, laying them in order on the ground.

I pretended not to watch.

I watched.

During lunch the graduate team asked questions.

"Hey, Dr. Gart, what's happening on Six?"

Gart put a pleased look on her face. "Actually," she said, "it's entirely possible that a much smaller complex lies buried within Structure Six. Antonio's men are beginning an exposure of the southeast wall to check it out."

I listened with interest, wondering how far she'd take the truth.

The boy with chin hairs spoke. "What makes you think there might be a smaller complex inside, Dr. Gart?"

"The vertical exposure shows the possibility of a space inside."

"That's awesome!" The girl who still needed clothes was exuberant. "A smaller complex, like . . . a burial chamber?"

There was a general flash of energy, a surge of excitement. Dr. Gart answered sternly, like a schoolmaster disciplining students. "We don't know if it's a burial chamber." Her efforts went unheeded.

"Can we go down the excavation and look?"

"Is there a hole big enough to actually see a room?"

"Is there a sarcophagus?"

"Oh man, if there's a mummy this'll be the find of the century!"

Gart had to raise her voice to be heard. "Everybody settle down! You will all stay away until I call you, understand?" Moans of disappointment prompted her to add, "If we break through, you'll be the first to know. Now, everyone, back to work."

She turned away without looking at me. Obviously, she'd made her decision and didn't want to discuss it. Whatever she was doing, it didn't include closing the site until other experienced professionals could be consulted. I settled myself at the artifact table in a position where I could keep a close eye on the southeast corner of Structure Six.

They shoveled all day in the slow, methodical, acceptable techniques of large exposures. About four in the afternoon I heard cheering and saw Dr. Gart climb on one of the facing blocks. Antonio and his men assembled for what looked like a speech and I decided to stroll in that direction, keeping myself at the back of the small crowd. Dr. Gart smiled above them, Antonio by her side ready to translate.

"Felicitaciones, amigos!" she said. The men nodded

their heads at the friendly congratulations. Then she switched to English.

"You've worked hard today. We've found the room."

Antonio translated. The men erupted with whoops and shouts. I scanned the excavation until I saw, barely jutting from the west part of the wall, a dressed rock that looked like a cornerstone. The room seemed to be positioned underneath the lower east staging area.

"This is an important discovery and we all deserve a break. Take the rest of the day off. In fact, take tomorrow off, too . . . with pay! Come back day after tomorrow and we'll open the chamber."

Antonio said the words in Spanish as the men looked at each other, puzzled at leaving when they were so close to their goal. But a free day with pay put smiles on their faces. Antonio caught my eye and made the slightest shrug of his shoulders. I made a pointed stare at the spot indicating an internal space. Gart saw the exchange and spoke quickly, "Rapido! Vayan a casa a celebrar." The men hurried down the path that would take them to their boats and villages. It was another "go home early" order. What was she up to?

During the commotion, Gart's team of graduate students wandered over, unable to wait for a formal invitation. Gart headed them off before they could see what I had seen.

"It's a holiday!" she said. "Go play some basketball on an ancient ball court and listen to your terrible music. Just make sure you're far enough away that I don't have to hear it." Her students grinned at the comment. "After that, go relax, read a novel, or anything that isn't about archaeology, wash your hair, get together and sing songs." She exuded charm. "I'll prepare dinner tonight." There were some cheers and Gart shooed them off like an indulgent parent, telling them to "have a good time," and "If you show up here, you'll get heavy labor."

I stayed.

"Well, Dr. Howard?" She had no smile for me. I had become the big bad wolf. I huffed and puffed.

"What are you up to, Dr. Gart?"

"Actually, that's none of your business. I've announced some free time, so use it."

In a bolt of realization, I knew she planned to take the light herself. Something in my expression must have tipped her off in that wordless language that passes between people.

She stiffened. "*Doctor* Howard," she said, with the emphasis on "doctor," "I have the authority to order you off this site."

"*Doctor* Gart," I replied, also emphasizing "doctor," "You can't order me off because Antonio is gone and I'm stuck here. If you're planning to break into the chamber and take whatever's shining, I'm in your way."

"Are you always this meddlesome?"

"Yes. But I'm not always this nice."

She considered me, her look saying she wished I'd never come to Lowry's Bight. "You told me you'd support my decision."

"But I expected you to be professional and responsible. You can't interfere with scientific evidence, regardless of the consequences."

"A lot of scientists do what's needed to protect established truth. Howard Vyse might be a good example."

I remembered the rumors. Vyse wanted proof that the Giza pyramid was built by Khufu. Just before his funding ran out, he discovered the right name scribbled in an inaccessible quarry mark. It was very convenient.

Gart added more fuel. "The Laetoli footprints are modern human, even though there were no humans three and a half million years ago. The only sane thing to do is ignore them until they can be explained."

It was a good example.

Gart had more. "Maybe you've forgotten Piltdown Man. He had to be manufactured to give evolution a kick-start. He was in the textbooks for fifty years, long enough to establish evolution as truth . . ."

"You've made your point," I said. "You're not in the best company, but there's a lot of it."

"A girl's gotta do what a girl's gotta do."

"So, you justify tampering with evidence to protect scientific status quo?"

"Whatever's in there, I won't let it destroy my work here. This place is unique. I've made the decision to save Cerros. Are you with me?"

I thought if I stayed close, I could have some influence. "I'll do what I can to help you."

"Good," she said. "I'm going for the backhoe."

"Backhoe! You can't use a back . . ."

"Are you with me or not?"

"I can't ravish an ancient . . ."

"Are you with me or not?"

"I'm not. You can't do this."

"I can and I will. Let me remind you, yet again, that I am in charge of this project, and short of a physical fistfight, which I'd win, you can't stop me. So, get out of the way. I have to move while everybody's gone."

"Please, Doctor Gart . . . Susan. Consider the enormity of what you're doing."

She brushed past me and headed for an open shelter where the backhoe was stored. From the opposite side of the clearing came raucous music and loud shouts. The students had moved toward the south ball court to test their skill with an old soccer ball someone had brought. I had to give Gart credit for good planning. With a little luck, the loud blare of music and games would cover noise from the backhoe.

As she rode the small machine to the crumbling eastern part of the ruins, she idled it for a moment. I figured this was my last chance to stop the desecration.

"I know you understand," I said, "that once you remove whatever it is, be it flashlight or alien technology, you can't put it back . . ."

Gart interrupted. "That's right, so there's no point reporting it." She glared at me pointedly, then continued. "I'd appreciate it if you wouldn't stand around and watch."

She was right. I couldn't stop her. I turned and walked slowly to my tent, dropped to my knees, and prayed fiercely to know what to do. Then I found my binoculars and spent the next half hour skulking behind a corner, watching Gart's progress, expecting God to intervene or give me inspiration. But the heavens were silent.

Gart didn't work on the west part of the wall, where the cornerstone was partially exposed, but rather on the opposite eastern side. Clever. The chamber would be close to the surface and she wouldn't have to disturb the men's excavation. Enough rubble existed at the east corner that the backhoe could add damage without too much shock. I could tell when she'd ruptured her way into the room. She jumped from the backhoe, scrambled to a rift in the pyramid wall, and crawled in headfirst. It was a stupid, dangerous thing to do. The whole structure could shift and bury her under a mountain of fill. But in sixty seconds she shot out of the fracture, slid to the machine, and filled the gap. Whatever she'd found inside must have fit in her pocket . . . first clue, smaller than a breadbox.

I held my head in my hand, considered the eternal loss, and grieved for the truth which would never be known. "God? Why didn't you help?" I whispered. At first I wasn't aware of the spot of warmth growing at the core of my body until it reached my shoulders. Then it had all my attention. "So," I thought to myself. "This is how God does it." I'd read about the process in Doctrine and Covenants 8. The warmth enveloped me in peace. It was all right. Everything was all right.

"Okay," I said to God. "If You don't care, I don't care."

As Gart drove the backhoe to its shed, I walked out to meet her.

"Do you need help with dinner?" I asked.

"As a matter of fact," she replied, "I do."

CHAPTER 18

D ay thirteen.
Gart gathered her team and drew their attention to the corner Antonio's men had uncovered, directing them away from the pile of rubble she'd created, which blended with the ruins on that side. She set her students digging like dentists with small picks and shovels, supervising their work, teaching them techniques. By lunch they had uncovered the bottom corner. Gart wanted to be absolutely sure of the orientation of the room.

The breach was made close to the floor in the afternoon. Each person took a turn peering beyond the perforation into a small chamber. It was dark, of course, highlighted by a lantern shoved into the opening and placed on a smooth surface. The smallest ray of sun from the far east corner traveled through the destruction of Gart's backhoe excavation. *Perfect,* I thought. *She can tell the men there was a hole in the outside wall.*

The lantern blinded us as it shed its scanty illumination across the floor. The room looked about eight-feet square. A stone altar rose four feet high, with a top platform about a foot square. There was nothing else: no coffin, no body, no treasure . . . no light.

The team discussed the kind of idol that must have perched on the altar, describing blood rituals the priest would have done. They agreed a passage led to the upper stage outside, but couldn't see through the shadows. Gart wouldn't allow enlargement of the opening because of danger. I supported her decision.

When all opinions had been aired, she ordered the opening closed, saying Antonio's men were undisciplined and would likely try to enter, a dangerous act. She would note the existence of the room in the season's report and leave official exploration for a time when precautions could be planned. The team carefully filled in the seventy-seven-meter excavation, leaving the outer blocks for the native workers to replace. When everyone left for dinner, the pyramid looked presentable.

I moved to the plaza and stared up at the two elaborate stages flanking the stairs, visualizing the spectacle that would have taken place. On the lower platform, drums, dancing, chanting, perhaps sacrifice, would have held the crowd in anticipation. Finally, when night was complete, at precisely the right moment, the priest would appear on the top stage with an unnatural, otherworldly light in his hand. The people would gasp, fall to their knees, and worship. Maybe they knew what they had. Maybe they didn't.

The evening drifted away indifferently. Dinner was in my honor. I gave a speech befitting the occasion, praised the work of the team, reported on my findings, corroborated dates, and commended Dr. Gart for her integrity. It went well.

That night I approached Gart's tent, encouraged by the propane lantern still burning within, and knocked on the side post.

"Come in," she said. I did.

The tent was organized and clean, no personal pictures or collections, a sterile place with a cot, two camp chairs, a small table, and a wood crate at the back wall, sturdy enough to sit on. A bright propane lamp sat on the table, spreading light and shadow as it hissed merrily. She stood and said nothing. It looked like I'd have to start.

"Tomorrow morning I'll go home."

"Yes. Thank you for your help here."

"I'd like to see it before I go."

"See what?"

"The light."

"There wasn't a light, just a pool of water reflecting the sun."

"Will that be your official story?"

"No. That's what I'll tell the men. My final report will mention the possibility of a chamber in Structure Six, to be examined later when safety measures can be implemented."

I looked at her for a moment, trying to decide how best to proceed. I had to be careful or the whole thing would slide through my fingers. Abruptly, I thought of James Marchant, the young man in China who had given me his Book of Mormon. I kept that copy home and traveled with an alternate, but his name gave me courage. I pulled up an extra camp chair and sat down, though I hadn't been invited.

"If I can describe it, can I see it?"

She arched one eyebrow.

I smiled. "I'll assume that's a yes." I leaned one elbow against the chair's flimsy arm to convey a casual attitude. She sat down and gave a slight tilt to her head, which would ordinarily be seen as noncommittal, but could also be interpreted as a definite go-ahead.

"It wasn't a penlight." I spoke with surety.

She gave no answer.

"And it wasn't a phosphorescent rock." I smiled disarmingly.

She didn't disarm.

My imagination and I blundered forward. It might have been one of the smooth globes of light produced by the prehistoric, technologically advanced society Mahi had described. But I didn't think so. For one thing, it was small enough to fit in Gart's pocket. No, this was one of the Jaredite stones. I felt it like a prickle on my spine. Moriancumer had smelted it with the tools and skills he'd used to build eight ships. But lights from rocks were an afterthought, and he probably didn't spend much time smoothing and polishing sixteen stones. I took a breath and a chance.

"It's like a crystal or a piece of glass." Here goes, I thought. "White, clear, transparent," that was a safe statement, straight out of the Book of Ether. "It's been formed with heat but not finished and polished, as if the maker hurried to produce it and didn't take time to smooth the edges. Uh . . ." I decided to add a little extra from Mahi's description. "It doesn't hurt your eyes to look directly at it and . . . it's cool to the touch. Am I right so far?"

"Close," she acknowledged.

Goody, goody. I forged ahead. "What I don't know is the size, though I expect it would fit in your hand."

I stopped.

She didn't respond. Finally, she said, "How do you know about lighted rocks?"

Bingo.

"I have a book that mentions lights from stones."

"You're kidding."

"I'm absolutely serious. In fact, I have it with me."

I could almost hear thoughts forming in her head because I'd had the same in China. She spoke the exact words.

"You carry around a book about shining stones?"

There was a moment of déjà vu, a transference to Mount T'ai Shan. I continued speaking the script.

"Yup. I always take it with me on trips."

I shifted. She shifted.

"Can I borrow it?"

"Tell you what," I said, repeating what James had once said to me. "If you promise to read it, I'll give it to you as a gift, a memory of this occasion and the importance of this site. Now, will you show me the light?"

"You're a weird lady," Gart said. She moved to the back of her tent, opened the wood crate, reached inside, and pulled out . . . a shoebox.

I broke out in a chuckle. "I thought you'd keep it in a jewel-studded reliquary."

"I always carry a shoebox," she smiled slightly. "It's a perfect size." She handed it to me.

I sat with the box on my lap, hesitant to open it, aware that four thousand years of sacred history was inside. Then I lifted the lid.

I felt . . . disappointed.

"It's just an old convoluted piece of glass," I said. "Why isn't it glowing?" I picked the thing up. It had an old, greenish tinge and looked about the size of a chicken egg, no heavier than a stone of those dimensions should be, maybe three ounces. The glass had a kidney shape with wrinkles, and a few worn or broken places created opaque spots. I studied its center, searching for signs of something unusual, even mechanical, but it was an ordinary rock. I glanced at Gart who looked amused.

"I noticed last night," she said, "that if another source of light is present, the glow fades. Watch what happens when I turn off the propane."

She did.

Darkness. Except . . .

The rock in my hand showed a tiny pinpoint of luminosity at the center, which quickly began to spread, as if the universe lived inside and it took a few light-seconds to reach the periphery. An electric sensation thrilled through me, and, suddenly, the tent was bathed in gold radiance. The rock in my hand remained cool. I gazed at it, awed by the impact of its reality.

So . . . we meet at last, I said mentally to the object resting on my palm. *Where have you been during eternity? What have you seen? I wish you could tell me the wonder of what's happened to you, the ancient prophets who have held you. You've been touched by the finger of God. You shine with His eternal light. What marvelous . . .*

"That's enough," Gart said, and she struck a match to relight her lamp. The glowing of the stone diminished.

"All right," she said, as she replaced her stolen artifact in its plebian container. "You've seen it. There was some mention of a book?"

"Are you sure you want to read it?"

"Dr. Howard," she said. "Indulge me."

I went to my tent, found my copy of the Book of Mormon, opened it and wrote: "This book belongs to Matt Howard. If found, do not return. Keep it. Read it. Tell me what you think." Then I added my address and phone number and returned to Gart's lodgings.

When I handed over my Book of Mormon, her reaction was predictable.

"What's this? A joke?"

"I assure you, it's serious. It does mention light-giving stones."

"Well," she snorted in disgust. "I'm not worried anymore you'll tell someone you saw a light in a pyramid. I'll just say you're a Mormon and delusional. Your word against mine won't be a problem."

"That's true," I said, good-naturedly. "What will you do with the light?"

Gart spoke with some humor, as if we were sparring partners in practice. "You can't have it, if that's what you're hinting at."

"Maybe I can't have it, but you can't show it to anyone." I smiled. "So it's an impasse. That's why, someday, you'll want to read my book and find out what it says about your rock."

"Can you mark the place for me?"

"No. You'll have to read it all."

She sighed.

It was time to leave.

"Goodnight, Dr. Gart. The adventure has been worth the trouble."

"Dr. Howard?" she said as I zipped open the door flap. "What will you say about Cerros?"

I gave her a crooked grin. "I'll tell people to bring mosquito repellent. A *lot* of mosquito repellent."

I closed the fold and took a couple of steps when she opened it again.

"Dr. Howard?" she called out. I stopped, turned, and she continued. "If I send my old archaeology book to you, the one you wrote, would you autograph it for me?"

"It would be a pleasure." I faded into the night.

CHAPTER 19

There was plenty of time to think. Antonio hadn't yet oiled his boat's engine, so the clatter prevented talking. He and his men had stood earlier in the morning sun to hear the water-in-the-chamber-reflecting-sun answer that Gart produced. He'd asked me about it while we packed my equipment. My obligation not to undermine Gart prevented me from contradicting her story, but Antonio worked out his own code and trapped me into a semblance of the truth.

"The light . . . it was not from Ephron."

"No."

"It was a different light."

"Hey, Antonio, would you hand me those tent pegs?"

"You do not answer. It mean *jes.*"

"Not necessarily, Antonio. Don't jump . . ."

"She took the light, *jes?*"

"Antonio! Stop that!"

"You do not say no. That mean *jes.*"

"Look, you've heard what Dr. Gart said about a room with water. I can't tell you something different."

"You tell me different by what you do not say."

"Can you roll the canvas tighter?"

"You see how you tell me?"

"Antonio, I wish you wouldn't push this . . ."

"It was very, very old, not from these times, no?"

"No. I mean yes. I mean . . . Antonio! I can't talk about it."

"Please, Señora Doctor, only one more. What it is look like?"

He deserved an answer. I searched the ground, found a rock about the size of a hen egg, and threw it to him.

"Glass," I said. A cryptic clue. He looked puzzled.

"A rock of glass?"

"I think we're packed up and ready for the path home."

"That is *jes*," he grinned. "A rock of glass."

I growled my frustration.

He put the rock in his pocket.

My taxi driver was waiting at the village of Chunox. Antonio and I said our good-byes, and I decided to tell him one more thing.

"It was made by God," I said. I knew Antonio was a good Catholic and would appreciate that information.

"Of course," he said as he shook my hand. "Only God could do this thing."

The flight to Chicago seemed surreal, with my mind still connected to the jungle below. Cerros had been populated, based on amount and distribution of pottery, during the Ixtabai phase, dating about 300 BC. Construction of the monuments and use of the ceremonial center occurred during the Tulix phase, from 50 BC to AD 150. Then, suddenly, the place was abandoned.

Preservation of Structure Six, with its giant masks still

showing color, was due to its deliberate burial before the people left. Why didn't they take the light with them? The answer to that would be found in the question of why they left to begin with, and why they never returned. The mystery of Cerros couldn't be solved without understanding that someone had introduced a supernatural light and Cerros had been constructed around it. Dr. Gart would know but could never talk about it, which served her right. I giggled uncharitably.

I wondered if the light in Brazil was another Jaredite stone, or if the squat tower housed a globe like the light in the Tibetan cave. Mahi had said one of the repositories for that civilization was in South America, so Brazil fit the requirement. But a squat tower didn't strike me as big enough to hold the large machinery of an advanced civilization. Percy Fawcett's description of houses lighted by "stars" sounded more like the small stones of the Jaredites. It still hurt to think of Brazil, but there was comfort in believing that death had been overcome and Ram and Pop survived somewhere.

Mount T'ai Shan in China, where the lights were presumably produced, brought more questions. Did the Jaredites begin their crossing from that point? Where did they land? Were they what we now call the Olmec civilization?

The talisman light of Alexander the Great seemed likely to be a Jaredite stone, small enough to be carried in the conqueror's belt. How Alexander got the stone might be tied up in ancient trade routes. Old Greek accounts claim that ships in 1800 BC left Greek shores on a three-year voyage, returning with fine quality copper. Jaredite copper? Perhaps one of those journeys brought back a rock that gave light. How can we ever know? All we have of

Jaredite history is what Ether wrote and Moroni abridged, a scant thirty-one pages covering 1,500 years of a lost civilization.

I couldn't make the parts fit.

In the end, it didn't matter.

Marisa met me in Chicago. There was a certain coolness, and I was glad I'd gone to Belize first so that conversation in the car could have a focus. I told her about the ceremonial center, the insects that bite, trees that burn, men who toil, the graduate students, Dr. Gart, and Antonio . . . no mention of the light. The freeze between us had thawed by the time we reached her apartment.

She proudly took me to see her beautiful creation, greater than an ancient center in Belize, finer than sculpted jade or gold, exquisite as porcelain, more valuable than platinum:

Annie.

The little round face looked up at us from her place in the crib. She had dark eyes, one deep dimple, and a tiny mouth which moved up and down. There was no hair to speak of, but what little existed had been combed in one direction and lacquered down. A small pink bow somehow stuck to the side of her head. I looked for a hairpin, but there was nothing to fasten it to.

"How on earth do you keep a bow in that baby's hair?"

"Karo syrup."

Who would'a guessed. "Aren't you concerned it will attract ants and they'll crawl all over and bite her?"

"Mom! That's so gross. You've spent too much time in the jungle."

"Forgive me," I said. "It's ingenious. I never would have thought to pour syrup on a baby and stick a ribbon in it."

I looked at the child.

Marisa looked at me.

"Marisa," I said, "I wonder if I could have a moment alone with my beautiful granddaughter?"

Marisa was taken by surprise but gracefully recovered. "Of course, Mom. I'll leave you two to get acquainted."

I smiled down and said hello to Annie. Her miniscule fist wrapped itself around my finger, and I felt the warmth of her little life.

"So . . . we meet at last," I spoke aloud to the child. "Where have you been during eternity? I wish you could share with me the wonder of what's happened to you. But by the time you learn to talk, the veil will be closed. Maybe someday your mother will let me tell you about the plan of our Heavenly Father to make us perfect like He is. Of course, you're perfect now. You've been touched by the finger of God."

I reached under my granddaughter and placed her gently on my shoulder. Her head snuggled in the crook of my neck and I whispered in her ear, "You shine with His eternal light."

A wet warmth spread across my neck to dribble under my shirt and down my back. The smell of sour milk was accompanied by Annie's soft coo.

Oh, well.

Epilogue

A year later I learned that it was Joseph Smith who had revealed the full name of the Jaredite leader who climbed Mount Shelem and returned with lighted rocks: Mahonri Moriancumer. I empathized with the guy. We both had unreasonable names. No wonder the ancient scribes decided to write him in as "the brother of Jared."

Not long after, a lady in the Relief Society cornered me by my chair.

"I thought, since you teach archaeology, you'd be interested in knowing that an early Church member in Nauvoo found one of the Jaredite stones."

"Really?" I had a talent for understatement. "I think Jaredite stones are a fascinating subject."

"It was a man named Edwin Rushton. He dug it up, carried it with him across the plains, and his family still has it."

I nodded. I might have even smiled as I said softly, "I'll bet they keep it in a shoebox."

She didn't skip a beat. "Isn't that the most exciting thing," she enthused. "It proves the Book of Mormon."

"The Book of Mormon doesn't need proof," I said. "People believe it or they don't. A rock won't convince anybody, even if it shines." I realized I was pouring wet negativity all over her enthusiasm and amended my statement. "I, however, am enormously excited in knowing there's a real Jaredite stone somewhere in . . . uh . . ."

"It's in Manti, Utah. The family won't let anyone see it, though. They don't want crowds of people lining up at their front door."

"Does it still shine?"

"I don't know."

"How big is it?"

"I don't know."

"Who told you about it?"

"Someone in my walking group."

Her ridiculous story had the feel of truth about it.

So, I thought. *Five out of sixteen, scattered across the western hemisphere. One in Nauvoo, one in Belize, one or more in Brazil, and one in the belt of Alexander the Great. If you count the light mentioned by Oliver Cowdery in the cave at Cumorah, it totals five shining rocks. A portion of a miracle created for a group of people traveling in darkness.*

I turned my attention back to the well-meaning lady in front of me.

"Thank you for telling me." I was sincere. "If you learn any more, be sure and let me know."

I really wasn't looking. The lights of Mahonri Moriancumer had been a miracle 4,000 years ago, but no greater than the restoration of the gospel in our time. God still does miracles for people who need light.

People like me, for example.

$\mathcal{A} \upsilon \mathcal{T} \mathcal{H} O R's \mathcal{N} O \mathcal{T} \mathcal{E}$

This book is fiction, influenced by the work and research of those who write non-fiction.

Thirty years ago I attended a class taught by Hugh Nibley, in which I heard for the first time that people before the flood possessed a high civilization. "They tried to advance themselves beyond God through technology," he said. "They had the advanced sciences. They had engineering projects to control nature. It was their undoing."

Years later I came across Graham Hancock's *Fingerprints of the Gods*, detailing evidence of a prehistoric advanced civilization. Not long after, *The Cave of the Ancients*, written by the Tibetan Monk T. Lobsang Rampa, came into my hands. He said he had seen a cave in Tibet containing the technological wonders of a culture drowned during a cataclysmic flood. Part of his description included lights hanging from the ceiling that never went out. Thus, the beginnings of this novel were formed.

Scenes in Bangkok, Thailand, include my personal experience. Much of the detail for the Chinese section of the story was gleaned from three sources: John Heinerman's *Hidden Treasures of Ancient American*

Cultures; my observations of China; and the scholarly works of Hugh Nibley in *There Were Jaredites.* Nibley is also the source of information that Alexander the Great had a shining stone.

The Belize site of Cerros is described from my visit to that area, plus information included in the archaeology reports from that site. Accounts of a light inside a pyramid come from the villagers of Chunox. The description of the Jaredite stone is supplied by Heinerman's book, and the idea that the stone dims in the presence of other light comes from Nibley's sources.

Genuine archaeologists will recognize that my familiarity with their profession is limited. I repeat, this book is fiction.

Finally, the Book of Mormon, most assuredly not fiction, is the major impetus for this work.

ABOUT THE AUTHOR

Phyllis Gunderson graduated from Brigham Young University with a master's degree in Communications and a master's minor in ancient scriptures. Travels to India, Belize, China, and Egypt, plus missions to Thailand and Cambodia, gave background for this story. Phyllis served three missions for the LDS Church and has eight children and thirty-four grandchildren.

EMIL' KEME (aka Emilio del Valle Escalante) is an Indigenous K'iche' Maya scholar. He teaches at the University of North Carolina, Chapel Hill, and is the author of *Maya Nationalisms and Postcolonial Challenges in Guatemala*. In 2020, he was awarded Cuba's Casa de las Américas literary criticism prize for the Spanish edition of *Le Maya Q'atzij / Our Maya Word*.